D1008353

Transforming the Way We Work

The Power of the Collaborative Workplace

Edward M. Marshall, Ph.D.

amacom

American Management Association

New York • Atlanta • Boston • Chicago • Kansas City • San Francisco • Washington, D.C.
Brussels • Mexico City • Tokyo • Toronto

Library of Congress Cataloging-in-Publication Data

Marshall, Edward M., 1946–
    Transforming the way we work : the power of the collaborative workplace / Edward M. Marshall.
    p.   cm.
    Includes bibliographical references and index.
    ISBN 0-8144-0255-0
    1. Work ethic.   2. Cooperativeness.   3. Management.   I. Title.
HD4905.M35   1995
306.3'613—dc20   94-48388
                                             CIP

THE COLLABORATIVE WORK ETHIC, THE COLLABORATIVE WORKPLACE AND DESIGN, CREATING A COLLABORATIVE WORK ENVIRONMENT, THE COLLABORATIVE METHOD, and THE WORKPLACE CULTURE INDEX are registered with the U.S. Patent Office or are pending registration.

Printing number

10 9 8 7 6 5 4 3 2 1

Contents

Preface

What would the world of work be like if we all truly respected one another? How effective would our workplaces be if we all knew how to collaborate? How efficient might we become as businesses if we were able to tap into the hidden productivity of the workforce? How successful might we become as a nation if we learned how to use the power and creativity of our workplaces for competitive advantage and world leadership?

I have often thought that the human condition was one of conflict by design, and that the cosmic joke was that we would never be able to find peace within and among ourselves. I have not been willing to succumb to that conclusion. There is a way out—the purpose of our journey in life is to discover it.

As we approach the 21st century, I believe we are at a critical fork in the road. We face a fundamental paradox of the human condition. On the one hand, we are increasing our capacity to liberate ourselves from the forces that have enslaved us all for generations: poverty, war, famine, and disease. On the other hand, we remain victims of those same forces.

The Cold War is over, and warring nations are finding ways to talk with one another, and yet new crises seem to emerge almost as quickly as old ones are concluded. The technological revolution is giving us more time to think creatively about ourselves and our world, and yet our innovations and patterns of consumption threaten the very fabric of our fragile ecosystem. The social revolution has created new levels of personal freedom and awareness, but as the family unit and our sense of community are damaged, we are learning the critical importance of basic values as an anchor for stability. The marvel of American market economics has generated unprecedented wealth and a model for progress which is the envy of the world, and yet almost half of our population is illiterate, the gap between rich and poor is increasing, and we have hungry and homeless people sleeping on grates one block from the White House. In the workplace, the efficiency of the Industrial Age machine-model of organization produces fear and compliance in the Information Age, sapping the creativity, productivity, and competitive edge of the workforce.

Do we have the capacity to deal with this paradox? Can we transcend our own self-imposed limitations? Can we see the cosmic joke for what it is and learn to laugh at ourselves as we learn how to break through those limitations?

I believe we can and that we must, which is why I have written this book. I feel compelled to take this journey and to confront the pain I see in the workplace. With you, I am committed to discovering new ways to build and enhance our work relationships so that we can be honest and authentic with each other, learn to trust again, and transform work into a place where we can contribute, serve, learn, and grow.

So why the optimism? What makes me think that we can create trust in the workplace? With all the emphasis on cost reductions and downsizing, isn't the world of work just another dimension of the paradox? Is my optimism just another form of self-delusion? I do not think so.

Having survived polio at age one, I have come to understand the power of the struggle for life. I have learned that optimism is my way of coping with what could otherwise become an intolerable circumstance. I have learned that I am responsible for what happens to me; I cannot blame anyone else. And if this world disintegrates in front of me, it is my responsibility to do what I can to stop the process. I believe in the power of the life that God granted me and all of us, and I have a profound faith in our abilities as a people to survive and thrive in the face of enormous adversity—if we choose to do so. The critical issue is whether we will make the choice and become responsible for the outcome.

This book, then, is an expression of my optimism, a statement about the power of the life we can each breathe into our workplaces. In my work with hundreds of companies over the past two decades, I have consistently heard the lament of powerlessness: "I cannot change anything." We are only as powerless as we choose to be. We make choices all the time—to live or die, to forgive or hold a grudge, to build trust or to break it. Ultimately this book is about both choice and transcendence. The choice to be made here is to transcend our own notions about what is right and to discover a new way of working together that enables us all to win. The choice is for peace, stability, and abundance in our work life.

As we look at the paradox of the workplace, however, with all of its chaos and opportunity, will we choose to take full responsibility to alleviate the pain we see? Will we choose to change our own behavior so that others may succeed? Will we choose to give up old ways of doing things so that we may discover new perspectives, insights, and skills?

The Collaborative Workplace provides us a framework for making that choice. Grounded in a fundamental set of values that are central to our self-esteem, the Collaborative Workplace is ours to create and sustain. If we really believe that we have a fundamental right to respect, honor, dignity, and integrity at work, then we belong in the Collaborative Workplace. As we will see, this Workplace is a not a place per se, and is not the program-of-the-month. True collaboration is a way of life. It is an ethic and an organizing principle for how we lead and manage our businesses and organizations. It is the leading candidate for replacing hierarchy as the cultural foundation for how we organize our work.

We can create a Collaborative Workplace anywhere. As a cultural framework and way of working together, I have seen its methods and tools applied not only in offices and plants, but also in families, schools, fraternal organizations, and community groups. Collaboration truly empowers people because it provides a structured basis for building and nurturing mutual respect while ensuring responsibility and accountability. When people leave or are downsized out of their jobs, they take the Collaborative Workplace with them. It is portable. It lives in the heart.

In the workplace, collaboration is efficient. In fact, in the new world of work, it is perhaps the most efficient and effective way to organize our people, business processes, and resources. It is the most efficient form of organization because it builds mutual respect, trust, and integrity into our daily interactions. The Collaborative Workplace is responsible, accountable, and focused on the customer.

Collaboration brings civility into the workplace. It gives us a way to empower ourselves, provides a foundation for new work relationships in all kinds of settings, and enables us to resolve conflicts, disputes, and disagreements without compromising our individuality. Finally, collaboration provides a framework for integration of our home life with the workplace so that we can see ourselves as complete human beings.

Think of collaboration as a gyroscope. As a principle, methodology, and toolkit, it helps us maintain our balance and homeostasis as we face the paradox of the workplace and the chaos of the marketplace. As we experience the consequences and instability brought on by hierarchy as a way to lead and manage, our gyroscope provides us an alternative way of looking at the world.

It will not be an easy journey, but nothing really worth having has ever been easy. The journey to the Collaborative Workplace, however, allows us to operate on principle, enhance our self-respect, build trust among others, and keep our dignity. That is a journey worth taking.

This book is the product of a very personal journey. Motivated by my need to do what I can to stop the pain I see in organizations of all kinds, this manuscript is the result of thousands and thousands of hours of working with individuals and teams in companies who really want a new way to work. This is not an academic treatise, although it was informed by my formal training at the University of North Carolina at Chapel Hill, Syracuse University, the University of Vienna, and Claremont McKenna College.

I decided early on in my career to build theory out of reality. Hence, you will see very few footnotes. What I have done here is to distill my experience with hundreds of teams, executives, and their companies into a principle-based change methodology. This methodology is also more than theory. It has been applied in at least twenty-five company transformation processes in the past ten years, and it has worked. In fact, based on my work with E. I. du Pont de Nemours & Company, Inc., we were both awarded the first-ever team "Excellence in Organization Development Award" by the American Society for Training and Development. I then went on to apply the basic collaborative framework and develop new methods and tools in other companies, including Conoco, Bethlehem Steel, Marriott, Loral, and IBM. Time after time, the message kept coming back—collaboration is the way people naturally want to work together.

This book, then, is designed to bring definition to the collaborative way of work life. What you will find here is a road map to the Collaborative Workplace. Part I defines the cornerstones of collaboration—what it is, how it works, and what a Collaborative Workplace looks like. Part I then goes on to explore the powerful role played by the workplace culture in determining how well we work together and examines how changes in that culture can transform our relationships. You will see how the principle of collaboration applies to all aspects of the business—its customers, work processes, and organization systems—and learn that it is indeed possible to create such a workplace.

Part II presents a method that allows us to create and manage this workplace. As you will see, making the change is as much an art as it is a structured process. And even once it is in place, there are many ways that collaboration can be unraveled. Because it is a way of life and not a quick fix, the Collaborative Workplace becomes a place where we continue to learn about ourselves, our work, and each other.

We do have a choice. Let's start the journey.

Edward M. Marshall, Ph.D.
The Marshall Group
Chapel Hill, North Carolina

Acknowledgments

I dedicate this work to my sons, Adam and Jonathan, that you may grow up in a world where respect, trust, and peace are possible. I also dedicate this work to my wife, Elise, who has believed in me and consistently given me the encouragement to realize my dreams. I am blessed with a truly loving family.

This volume is also dedicated to all of our children, that you may find this planet a better place to live in the 21st century because we adults chose to heal the past and to put principles to work for your future. I hope we will succeed.

I would like to thank my three spiritual guides and coaches, who had faith and confidence in my abilities to do this work and to articulate this framework. Special thanks to Steven T. Miller, who started this journey with me in the late 1980s and helped me formulate and document the basic premises of the Collaborative Workplace. Also to Clifford Ehrlich, who has shown me that there is a pathway to the future and that the path is one of collaboration. To Raymond Aumiller I extend my appreciation for showing me the value of optimism and for his undaunting belief in me and this work.

I also owe a debt of gratitude to my intellectual mentors who gave me the theoretical precepts that helped frame many of the concepts and perspectives in this book: Warren Bennis, Steven Covey, Peter Drucker, Jacques Ellul, Talcott Parsons, Scott Peck, Edgar Schein, and Max Weber.

Special thanks must also go to the hundreds of teams at many companies who gave of themselves to discover a new way to work with each other. Without you, this book would have never happened. You brought dignity and respect to simple methods and tools and made them come alive in your own way. I would particularly like to thank Louise Bertsche, Walter Cox, John Dobel, George Fugere, Al Ginouves, Joe Gorsczycka, Paul Harjung, Robert Hayes, Morris Helbach, Bill Laughton, Scott Leigh, Audy Longaker, Pierce Quinlan, Geoffrey Rendall, Esther Schaeffer, Patricia Thomas, and John Vance.

I will forever be indebted to my editor, Adrienne Hickey, who, throughout this experience, has provided me the precise type of support I needed at just the right time, and who has given me the impetus to continually refine my thoughts and communicate them in a more precise and forceful manner.

Last, but certainly not least, my hat is off to my own collaborative teammates at The Marshall Group. They made the production of this manuscript possible. It is never easy to manage a consulting practice while writing a book, but Magdalena Hurwitz, Lorraine Osborne, and Debbie Pennington did so with grace, patience, and nurturing support.

A couple of reference notes are in order. First, throughout the book, I use a number of case examples from actual companies, which have been given fictitious names. The situations described, however, are real. Some situations are composites of case examples, but have been written in a way that does not detract from the points being made.

Second, there are a number of terms of art that also reflect proprietary products and services developed by The Marshall Group, Inc., of Chapel Hill, North Carolina. The service-marked products and services include: The Collaborative Work Ethic℠, The Collaborative Workplace and Design℠, Creating a Collaborative Work Environment®, The Collaborative Method℠, and the Workplace Culture Index℠. These servicemarks have been registered with the U.S. Patent Office or are pending approval, and should reflect that fact when used by others.

1

Collaboration: The Quest for the 21st-Century Workplace

The best way to predict the future is to create it.
—Peter Drucker

American business is undergoing its most profound transformation since the Industrial Revolution. But what are we transforming into? Chaos and instability infect many of our organizations as this process leaves us wondering what the future may hold. We know we must realign the very essence of the way we lead and manage the business organization, but to what?

Hierarchy, the cultural principle by which we have led and managed business for at least the past century, no longer seems practical or relevant. The basic covenant we have had with our organizations is broken. Jobs are being eliminated or totally redesigned. Employees are expected to behave in new and different ways, but often they do not have the skills to do so. The rungs on the career ladder are no longer well defined, and many wonder whether the concept of a career ladder even exists anymore. In the meantime, the cultural framework in which business operates continues to evolve. Where is it heading? What is the new cultural foundation that will guide us into the 21st century?

Everyone is familiar with the litany of external marketplace factors causing this chaos—global competition, technology, and demographic and political changes. These have resulted in the elimination of millions of jobs, drastic restructuring, and new business relationships. What we are much less clear about is what is going on with our people *inside* our companies and how we must now work together to face the new realities. How are our employees handling this chaos? How can we regain their loyalty, confidence, energy, and productivity? And assuming we get that energy back, how will we sustain their commitment as our companies continue to face unrelenting change?

There Is No Silver Bullet

Most of us are either in denial about the impact of all this change, do not know what to do, or are still trying to figure out how to get back in control. Unfortunately, the result so far has been more of the same, a potpourri of programs designed to change the structure of our workplaces but not their essence—their culture. Downsizing, reengineering, and restructuring programs have succeeded in altering the employment base and cost structure of our companies, but do not offer us a new cultural framework. One round of structural change often leads to another, with the focus almost exclusively on the cost side of the ledger. In fact, structural changes often produce precisely the opposite result than intended by increasing instability, fear, and reduced productivity. Programs that focus on organizational effectiveness, empowerment, total quality, and/or self-directed work teams have been a powerful new tool for change in some companies. In most instances, however, the underlying values by which these organizations are led have not changed, resulting in enormous internal conflict. Management is seen as not walking the talk, thereby undercutting the value and impact of these process-focused programs.

There is no silver bullet that will solve the complex of organizational issues we face. Without fundamental cultural change and the adoption of a new approach to leading and managing, American businesses will continue to experience significant difficulties in sustaining competitive advantage.

The 21st-Century Workplace

We have always looked to the future with a fairly high degree of hope and anticipation that things will get better. This may not be the case now. We know that the 21st-century workplace will be totally different from what it is now. We know we need a new cultural framework to guide us in the design and creation of that workplace. It must do more with less and adapt quickly to or anticipate change. It must be nonbureaucratic and passionately focused on the customer. The members of the workforce must be aligned with and own the strategic direction of the business, have trust-based work relationships, and be able to build value with one another and their customers. Leadership in the new workplace must be seen, not as a *job*, based on power and authority, but as a *function* based on principles, new people skills, and the ability to engage others in coming to consensus around critical decisions and problem solving. The resulting trust and productivity will provide the enterprise a clear competitive advantage.

The Missing Ingredient:
The Workplace Culture

We have been expertly trained to focus on organizational structure, systems, and programs, while most of us would admit that fully 70 percent of all our problems in business are people-related or culturally based. By targeting the structures of the workplace rather than its culture as we seek to transform a business, we tend to focus on the trees and miss the forest. Our business cultures reflect the core values and beliefs that drive our actions and behaviors and influence our relationships, both internally and with our customers. The culture of a workplace shows up in powerful ways in terms of commitment, quality and productivity, loyalty, satisfaction, and pride. It creates the standards, work style, and expectations by which our companies are defined. Our job is to engage that culture so that its best values emerge and flourish.

The organization as a whole must create a shared cultural

framework that will be powerful enough to replace hierarchy. That framework must not merely be a program or technique or a sophisticated new way to manipulate the future. On the contrary, it must be based on fundamental principles, enhance the stability of workplace relationships, help define the new covenant, and enable managers to use common sense in making business decisions.

What, then, constitutes this new cultural framework? What does the new workplace look like? How can we go about creating and sustaining it? Will the view be worth the climb?

What Is Collaboration?

In my action research and work with hundreds of companies over the past 25 years, seven core values have surfaced again and again as the basis for effective work relationships: respect for people; honor and integrity; ownership and alignment; consensus; full responsibility and accountability; trust-based relationships; and recognition and growth. These core values represent a cultural framework for the 21st-century organization, a framework that adds up to collaboration.

Collaboration is the premier candidate to replace hierarchy as the organizing principle for leading and managing the 21st-century workplace.

It is a way of life that enables us to meet our fundamental needs for self-esteem and mutual respect in the workplace.

It is a principle-based process of working together, which produces trust, integrity, and breakthrough results by building true consensus, ownership, and alignment in all aspects of the organization.

Put another way, collaboration is the way people naturally want to work.

As a leadership principle, I have seen collaboration work in a wide range of tough business and organizational situations, from strategic alliances and mergers that were breaking up to internal mergers between departments; from companies in high-technology industries to those in the service sector; from senior executives to front-line managers. This principle provides the basis for significant and permanent change—for people as well as for organizations. Collaboration provides the cornerstone for the creation and enhancement of the 21st-century workplace.

Here are several other ways to think about this critical process:

- *A total shift.* Collaboration is not a program, a technique, or a partial solution. It is a total shift in the way we work together, think about our customers, and behave toward one another in the workplace.

- *A new work ethic.* Collaboration provides long-term stability for the workplace because it is a work ethic that recognizes that work gets done through people; that people want and need to be valued; that any change must be owned by those implementing it if it is to be successful.

- *A common denominator for relationships.* Collaboration provides the common denominator for engaging all members of the workforce, since its core values and beliefs are the foundation for building trust-based relationships.

- *A decision-making framework.* Collaboration provides an approach to basing business and organizational decisions on principle rather than power or personality—whether those decisions are about strategy, customers, people, or systems. Collaboration helps us decide when and how to use any particular program or technique to improve performance and how to engage the workforce in its implementation; it is just as concerned with relationships and the company's reputation as it is with bottom-line results.

- *A set of methods and tools.* Collaboration also provides a set of methods and tools that help the workforce become aligned, take ownership of and responsibility for the success of the enterprise, and build an organizational system that produces sustained high performance.

Put simply, collaboration is an idea whose time has come.

When Are Collaborative Team-Based Organizations Appropriate?

The collaborative framework for organizing work relationships is appropriate in most organizational settings, although it does not work in every organization due in part to factors other than the merits of the collaborative approach to leading and managing. Some of the situations where the Collaborative Workplace is appropriate include the following:

- When human productivity is less than 80 percent
- When there has been a reorganization, an internal merger, or a restructuring, making it critical for the diverse cultures to be focused in a common direction
- When ownership of the business' strategic direction is essential to success
- When conflicts in relationships affect either productivity, customer focus, or competitive position
- When the company wants to refocus its energies on the customer and become a quality, high-performance business
- After the organization has gone through reengineering and it needs to reenergize the survivors
- When a joint venture or strategic alliance is formed and trust and candor are essential to their success—usually requiring some blending of divergent cultures and the development of collaborative work processes
- When experiences with other quality, self-management, or cross-functional teams have not yielded the expected results

Collaborative approaches to leading and managing, however, are not for everyone. There are a number of situations where this approach should either not be attempted or attempted with caution. In all of these situations there appears to be a common denominator: The fundamental values and beliefs of senior management are such that they do not accept that collaboration is the way in which they want their organizations to evolve; or they believe it is the wrong way to manage. In some instances, management may intellectually understand the need for collaboration, but does not yet know how to implement it. In this situation, the collaborative option can be pursued, but with caution, since there may not be a high level of commitment to see the process through. Other organizations where collaboration may not work are those that have win-lose as their rule, such as political bodies. While I believe that collaboration is the new organizing principle for organizations in the 21st century, it will not work in every organizational setting.

What Are the Benefits of Collaboration?

The early results from companies that have installed truly collaborative workplaces are substantial:

- Organizations collaborate internally to compete externally.
- Decisions are faster, of higher quality, and customer-driven.
- Decisions are made on the basis of principle rather than power or personality, resulting in greater buy-in and impact.
- The energy of the workforce is focused on the customer rather than on internal conflicts.
- Cycle time is substantially reduced and nonvalue-adding work eliminated.
- The productive capacity of the workforce doubles. In one case, this was achieved within 12 months.
- Strategic alliances that might have failed not only succeed, but build trust and produce extraordinary results.
- Return on investment increases dramatically. In one full-scale change process, return on investment exceeded 15:1.
- Span of control increases substantially. In one case, it went from 1:5 to 1:50.
- The workforce takes on full responsibility and accountabil-

ity for the success of the enterprise, to the point where some teams have downsized themselves.

- Conflict is reduced as work relationships open up and build trust.
- Collaborative mergers and alliances result in all members pulling in the same direction.
- The fear is gone—change is seen as a positive opportunity.
- The organization is self-sufficient in sustaining the ongoing development of the company.

What Is the Collaborative Workplace Like?

Think of your own organization and how it currently operates. If we were to take each major component of that organization and redesign it in accordance with the principle and values of collaboration, we would call that new organization a Collaborative Workplace. As Figure 1–1 shows, there are five core components. (Each component is addressed primarily in Part I.) The five core components are:

1. *Collaborative culture*—A set of core values that shape the behaviors and conduct of a business. (See Chapters 2 and 3.)
2. *Collaborative leadership*—A shared, situational *function*, rather than a mere hierarchy of *position*, that involves everyone in the organization. (See Chapter 4.)
3. *Strategic vision*—The guiding principles and overall goals of a customer-driven organization that is internally aligned and strategically focused on its unique and value-added role in the market. (See Chapter 5.)
4. *Collaborative team processes*—A set of nonbureaucratic work processes managed by collaborative teams of aligned professionals who take full responsibility for their success and learn new skills that enable them to become self-sufficient. (See Chapters 6 and 9.)
5. *Collaborative structure*—The realignment of a business's support systems (especially its information systems and human resources) to ensure the success of the Collaborative

Figure 1–1. The Collaborative Workplace.

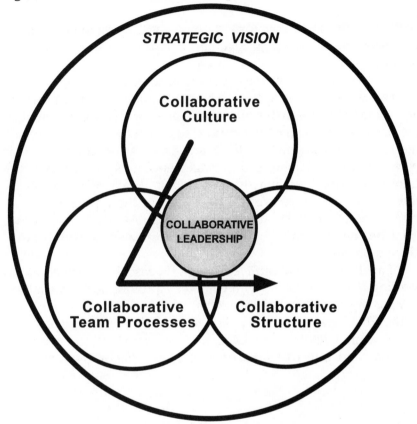

Workplace. Members of these internally focused groups see the rest of the organization as customers and focus on quality in all aspects of their work. (See Chapter 9.)

As a rule, the members of a Collaborative Workplace collaborate internally in order to compete externally. They are part of a highly productive and creative organization. Their energies are directed toward meeting customer needs, not toward fanning the flames of internal conflict.

How Do We Create a Collaborative Workplace?

Creating a Collaborative Workplace means making a commitment to a new way of working together. It is not a quick fix. It is an ongoing process. It is not for everyone.

Some organizations may not operate effectively if they employ the collaborative principle. Most organizations, however, benefit enormously from transforming their basis for leading and managing from hierarchy to collaboration. To do so, they have to be willing to stick it out through thick and thin as this century's basic paradigms of leadership and management undergo a fundamental transformation. Since by nature we do not like change—especially those of us who have excelled and risen to the top using the assumptions of the past—the challenge is substantial. How do we get from here to there? How do we implement a collaborative change process?

Part II, The Collaborative Change Process, is dedicated to answering these questions, with Chapter 7 providing the methodology for organizational change. Chapter 8 looks at the five phases of the Collaborative Method used to create a Collaborative Workplace, while Chapter 9 looks at what we must do to ensure the integrity and effective management of a collaborative organization.

Beginning the Journey

We live in extraordinary times that require extraordinary solutions to increasingly complex problems. The programs and techniques we have tried to date, including reengineering, downsizing, restructuring, total quality, and empowerment, have been helpful as far as they have gone. But now we must go much further in our thinking and behaving. We need to evolve personally and organizationally at a rate faster than the market, our competition, and our people may be willing to let us. We really have little choice.

In World War II, the United States built liberty ships at a phenomenally fast rate—faster than we thought possible. In 1957, when Russia put *Sputnik* into space, America was galvanized into meeting the threat and the challenge, creating a quantum leap in our technology. In 1992, when Iraq invaded Kuwait, we came together as a nation to win Desert Storm in a landmark 100 hours. In business today, we face a similar threat and challenge. The concept of collaboration allows organizations to move beyond quick fixes and single-focus programs and get back to basics about how to build a business. This involves being principle-driven, valuing our people, engaging our culture and productive energies, and working as a Collaborative Workplace. Collaboration offers us an opportunity to create the most efficient, effective, and productive organization we have ever seen.

The race to create the successful 21st-century workplace will require a victory of the human spirit over chaotic change and our own self-imposed limitations. To win this race, let us appreciate the most important asset we have: the values that already reside in each one of us and in the people we work with. The real task of leadership is to create a work environment in which these values can begin driving the enterprise.

If businesses want to thrive in the 21st century, they must seriously consider whether they are willing to detach themselves from the culture and comforts of the past to meet this challenge. The leaders and companies who do are likely to win. Those who don't—won't.

Let's look at how to do it.

Part I

Designing the Collaborative Workplace

2

The Collaborative Work Ethic

Matters of principle stand like a rock.
—Thomas Jefferson

The senior vice president for planning got up for his after-dinner speech and began by saying: "This business is not a democracy. We can't make all our decisions by consensus. But I do know I need to collaborate with you, and I want your buy-in to our plan to double the company's sales this next fiscal year." Without having realized it, this executive had just painted himself into a corner, using his position and authority to insist on collaboration, creating substantial confusion in the minds of his workforce about his leadership approach.

At a major utility, the workforce was adamant about the need for a culture change so that they could feel a greater sense of responsibility for the success of the business as they entered the era of deregulation. At the same time, supervisors were reengineering the company and eliminating 20 percent of the jobs.

These two situations symbolize the values conflict we are experiencing in our businesses. Most of us work in an environment characterized by what we could call a "culture war." We should not be surprised at this. The paradigm of hierarchy is collapsing and the new work ethic is not yet fully articulated or understood. We are in transition, evolving toward a new way of working together based on a new cultural framework.

This chapter explores the nature of the leadership styles that define the character of this culture war. We will consider the fundamental assumptions that govern how we like to work, and build a new cultural framework, the Collaborative Work Ethic, that can bring peace to the workplace.

The Culture Wars

We are in a values war with ourselves. Business leaders and members of the workforce have very different sets of beliefs and attitudes about how to lead and manage business in an era of chaotic change. The senior vice president mentioned above really wanted to *demand* buy-in; the audience wanted to collaborate. Throughout our business organizations, we are repeating this fundamental disconnect between the advocates of command-and-control and those pressing for more empowerment, collaboration, and accountability. (See Figure 2–1.) Just as management is in conflict, so too are members of the workforce, some of whom want to be told what to do, while others insist on significant participation in real decisions. No one is wrong or right; the question is, what process will work in the new realities?

The consequences of the culture wars are significant. At one blue-chip company, management estimates that it is spending over 50 percent of its time handling all the interpersonal conflicts that result from these value differences. In the short term, at the company level, advocates of the competing philosophies will fight it out in the trenches, consuming enormous amounts of energy and time in a process that detracts from their productivity and ability to focus on the customer. In the long run, companies that do not effectively resolve their culture wars may lose their direction, their customers, and the loyalty of their workforce. But what is the basis for resolution?

At the individual level, the culture wars take an enormous toll. Leaders and managers at all levels struggle daily to motivate their people and meet the bottom line, relying on their wits, common sense, political clout, and experience to guide them. Many business leaders become very conflicted as they try to balance efficiency and effectiveness and attempt to honor the traditional rules of the road in business while accommodating the growing

Figure 2–1. The culture wars.

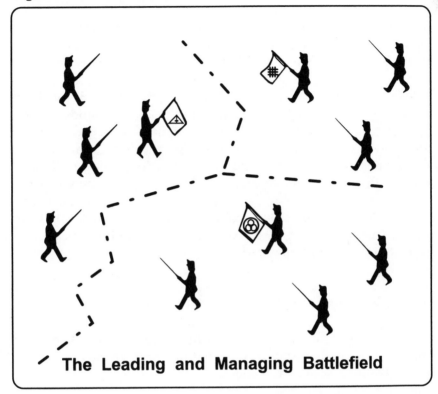

The Leading and Managing Battlefield

demands for more ownership in the workplace. Some leaders find themselves trapped in a no-man's-land between these competing value systems, not because they deliberately choose to be there, but because they are trying to bridge the culture gap between the paradigm called hierarchy they live in and the requirements of a more collaborative workplace.

In an environment of values conflict, how should decisions be made? Should we centralize or decentralize? Empower people or hold them accountable? Engage them in reengineering the business or keep them out of it? Should we focus on cost cutting to improve the bottom line and eliminate jobs? Or should we focus on increasing the productivity and long-term value of our people?

What should be the value system upon which any of these choices are made? What is our framework?

There is usually no clear answer. All too often, "might makes right," and cultural warfare increases as a natural part of our daily work. The culture war is fundamentally a conflict between traditional values and emerging values, between the old rules and the rules yet to come. Cultural warfare can result in the basic displacement of people, disrupted careers, and the loss of confidence and productivity. Furthermore, it can result in a work environment where the workforce is confused about what principles are driving the organization and where the leaders feel compromised. To succeed in the new work environment, the values of a new cultural framework for leading and managing our business organizations need to be articulated. Our goal should be a framework that can help us mediate differences in the workplace and bring peace and focus to our business enterprises.

Competing Values in the Culture Wars

Our business values are played out in the behaviors and styles of our business leaders and are reflected in their company cultures. I have identified seven basic styles.

The Rugged Individualist

The Maine lobsterman is a symbol of the rugged individualist in our society. Out there by himself in his boat, testing his will against the tides and the seas, the lobsterman sets and hauls hundreds of traps, trying to make a meager living and loving the sea. Dick is such a lobsterman and prides himself on being a rugged individualist. He talks about how important his independence is to him, and yet Dick belongs to a fisherman's cooperative, joins a team of four other lobstermen every other night to go seining for bait, and shares nets and the proceeds of his endeavors. So which is he: a rugged individualist or a team player? Perhaps both.

In business, the entrepreneur is a rugged individualist—independent, creative, and fiercely competitive. We admire entrepreneurs for their creativity, their ego strength, and their assertiveness. In our past, this cultural attribute was represented by the pioneer, the gold miner, and the farmer who staked out a patch of land. At the turn of the century it was the inventor, the industrialist, and the financial wizard: Alexander Graham Bell, Thomas Alva Edison, Andrew Carnegie, Henry Ford, John D. Rockefeller, and the other captains of industry who created the modern-day industrial dynamo. Today's rugged individualists tend to be found in the vanguard of such fields as biotechnology, computer software, and international business—people known for their creative daring and/or corporate know-how.

The Team Player

Dean Smith, coach of the Tar Heel basketball team at the University of North Carolina at Chapel Hill, has gained a national reputation for his abilities both on and off the basketball court. The team's championship record can be attributed to the value Smith places on true teamwork: playing freshmen in big national games rather than seating them on the bench to watch; establishing clear ground rules; and rotating his players to meet the competitive challenges in the game. Smith is an excellent strategist. But he is primarily known for the way he cares about his team members and cultivates their mutual support. This is not a team dependent on a few stars, but a star team with a deep bench that can usually outlast the competition. In many respects, Dean Smith's team is an excellent metaphor for the new corporation—it is collaborative internally in order to compete externally.

The team-player side of our national character represents a very different set of values—cooperation, collaboration, subordination of ego to the good of the whole, rewards for the group rather than for the individual, and situational leadership. There are many teams, however, that do not exhibit these behaviors, and while they might win a single season, they usually do not win consistently over the long term.

In business the team player is highly valued but usually unrecognized. Almost by definition, individuals on successful business teams are not well known. The paradox many businesses face in creating a team-based structure is that they want to capitalize on the strength of the team, but also want strong individual players or stars who will produce superior results. Sometimes the stars need to subordinate their individual success to the success of the team—"all for one and one for all."

The Autocrat

A very successful executive of a large corporation was well known for his regal manner and trappings of power. He used to come to work every day in a chauffeured limousine, wearing a white linen suit with a red rose in his lapel, and followed by a small entourage. In the course of creating his new corporate headquarters, he actually had the builders reset the foundation so that he could see a particular skyline from his corner office. At staff meetings he told his business leaders what to focus on; there was virtually no two-way or group communication.

Our cultural heritage values the autocratic leader who gets things done, demonstrates the gift of command, and achieves high levels of efficiency—the so-called heroic leader. The military is one place where the authority of the commander is expected, respected, and required. We certainly do not want a general asking the troops to vote on whether or not to take a hill. In business, the autocrat exercises command-and-control, provides a clear direction with little, if any, consultation, and personally rallies the troops to a new cause. Sometimes it works, but more often it does not.

In the military, there are extraordinary leaders—historic figures like Dwight D. Eisenhower, George S. Patton, and Douglas MacArthur—who command this respect. But in business, admiration for such leaders is more limited. Often the imperial leader's perks and idiosyncrasies begin to take precedence over the goals of the enterprise and lead to a downfall. Our regal executive, for instance, was ultimately relieved of his duties by a board whose members considered him arrogant and oblivious to the concerns of his workforce.

The Democrat

We also have a very strong democratic tradition in our culture, one that provides an equally compelling framework for the business high levels of conflict among their service providers. All they wanted was a high-quality product.

With an internal focus on competing against each other, the company was soon eclipsed by emerging but powerful global competitors. It did not even see them coming and got caught short. Because its hierarchical system could not respond quickly enough, there was a 10 percent loss of market share within three years.

We honor and cherish competition in all aspects of our culture. It is about winning and losing. Our children grow up rooting for their teams, and as adults continue the practice. We understand there are excesses and costs, but that is the price to be paid for competition, which is viewed as the best way to achieve excellence.

Competition is not all bad. What *is* important is who the object of the competition is, and how you play the game. Integrity, skill, and hard work are the hallmarks of the true competitors. Certainly dishonest or questionable business practices designed to disable the competition, such as corporate espionage, would not meet these standards.

Competition can be downright self-defeating when it is used as an internal organizing principle that pits the workers in the business against each other and management. There is a major consulting firm that has as its *modus operandi* that consultants receive their bonuses based on how much business they individually bring in. Among the results of this practice have been the theft by one consultant of another's clients, the withholding of valuable information, turf wars, and isolation. The company as a whole has been successful, but it could be much more so if its workers were pulling together toward a common goal.

The Bottom-Line Driver

In a $3-billion financial services firm, the senior executives are rewarded only for bottom-line results. Nothing else matters. Staff meetings are nonexistent. There is an intolerance for process. The only measures worth considering are financial ones.

In an information systems business, the reengineering effort has been successful at stripping out redundancies and reducing cycle time as well as 30 percent of the short-term costs. But a sur-

manager. As our dinner speaker pointed out, we are not going
vote on every decision that comes up, but we do need the suppc
and buy-in of most of the workforce if key business objectives a
to be successfully achieved. But do we need the buy-in of all t
members? The democrat will tend to seek out opinions, partic
larly those of people who are influential. But the decisions are us
ally made by an informal vote involving some compromise th
ensures the support of the key players while losing the suppc
of others.

Sometimes the values of democracy and autocracy get cross
and create confusion. In one high-technology company, the ne
vice president was given his orders by the board of directors. F
was to get the internal organization straightened out and chart
new strategic direction. He set to work, knowing what strateg
direction the business needed to take, but he wanted buy-in fro
the workforce. So he engaged the staff in a four-month strateg
participation extravaganza, focusing all its energies on coming u
with a new direction. In fact, the direction had already been se
but he wanted to create the appearance that everyone had bougl
in. Some of the staff had already figured out the game plan, reali
ing that this process amounted to nothing more than a six-mon
notice that their jobs were going to be terminated. Trust for seni
management dropped and the workforce realized they had be
manipulated. Productivity dropped, and top professionals beg
to leave the company. The attempt to camouflage the autocrat w
the democrat simply did not work.

The Competitor

At one Fortune 100 company, the wisdom for a time was that
similar production facilities at different locations should com
against each other, thereby cutting costs and producing a hig
quality product. For 20 years these two facilities competed, se
up their own information, finance, human resource, produc
quality, and safety systems. The prevailing attitude was to wi
almost-any-price, and that is exactly what happened. Costs
up because so many systems were duplicated. There was ani
ity among the workers. The customers were bewildered b

vey of the workforce has found that 65 percent of the members are angry at management for its heavy-handed approach and are fearful for their futures. Productivity has lagged significantly. Clearly, the bottom line involves more than short-term financial results.

Our culture rewards the bottom-line driver. Most businesses operate with a 90-day mentality, maximizing shareholder value in the short term even if it means sacrificing long-term productivity. In cultures like this, everything is reduced to a financial equation, and the value of relationships and work processes is subordinated to the economic formula. Often, however, workforce needs, psychology, and interpersonal dynamics eventually work to undermine the financial goals.

The Consensus Leader

The group vice president for a transportation industry company was well known for his multiday staff meetings every quarter. As members tried to get consensus, the meetings dragged on for hours. Some members thought this process was essential. Others saw little value in it and stopped going to meetings. The net result was a loss of alignment among the top managers, lost team synergy, and reduced value for the company's objectives.

Consensus is an often-used term that is misunderstood and misapplied in business settings. Our culture does not value consensus; it values either majority rule or top-down autocracy. At the same time, however, when asked what decision-making rule they would agree to use, most teams will choose consensus. Herein lies a paradox. We want consensus but do not know how to reach it effectively and efficiently. Consensus, if effectively developed, speaks to our need for respect, being valued, accountability and teamwork.

In many organizations, several of these styles exist side by side, adding to our cultural confusion. In one information systems company, the manager firmly believed that her group and the entire company ought to become more consensus-based in order to achieve greater efficiency and customer service. Her vice president, however, was an autocrat. Every time the manager tried to move her organization toward team-based decisions, she was overruled. Within a year, she had moved to another company, and her unit went through another 18 months of instability and lowered productivity.

The Working Assumptions Underlying Collaboration

Culture wars sap the energies of our people and our companies. We end up spending too much time managing internal conflicts—time that would be better spent meeting the needs of our customers. To reconcile these cultural differences and build a long-term foundation for high performance, we need a new set of values to guide the organization as a whole—a new cultural framework. Without it, businesses will continue to struggle. The default position will likely be hierarchy.

The cornerstones of a new cultural framework include the principles of American culture (individual rights, freedom, and democracy); what it takes to run a successful business (profitability and satisfied customers); and a commitment to meeting the basic needs of the workforce. These workforce needs are closely related to six fundamental assumptions about human behavior:

1. *We get work done through people.* The only way work gets completed or decisions get made is through other people. No matter how much technology we have or how simple our work processes are, work is still done through people. They in turn work with other people or machines to get the job done. Unfortunately, in an era when work is being totally transformed, this basic premise is sometimes forgotten in favor of the technological fix, cost reductions, or structural changes as a way to solve business problems. One result is the reduced loyalty and productivity of the workforce.

2. *A successful business values its people.* There is no way around this. The people in any business are its greatest asset. They are an intellectual resource and an essential source of energy and commitment. Most members of the workforce are motivated either by

survival, fear, service, legacy, or recognition. The most successful businesses will be those that truly value their people, respect them, invest in them, recognize them, engage them, and provide a work environment that enables them to serve, contribute, and innovate. Most members of the workforce also want to be treated like adults and be given the opportunity to be responsible and accountable for the success of the business. Unfortunately, there is a management mind-set that views members of the workforce as expendable assets. Such a mind-set also believes that it is okay to break the psychological contract with their workers if it is financially expedient and that those workers should not be involved in critical business decisions.

3. *Successful change is owned by the workforce.* The extent to which any business will be able to adapt to constant change in the marketplace is directly proportional to the extent to which its workforce has psychological ownership of the enterprise. Since workforce members are ultimately the custodians of the business, their loyalty, commitment, customer focus, and pride will depend on their being actively engaged in the key decisions and processes that directly affect their work lives.

Most members of the workforce *want* to contribute and to see the business succeed. It is only natural. Management needs to capitalize on that desire and to provide financial and nonfinancial ways for them to buy in. This is particularly important when a significant organizational change is involved. Unfortunately, there is a strong view that change should be mandated. But leaders who impose solutions are more likely to lose the commitment and loyalty of their people. Who else knows the business better than those working on the front lines?

4. *A shared perception of reality is essential.* The success of any change process, short or long term, is a function of the degree to which the members of the organization share the same view of what the change should be, based on a shared perception of current realities. Since people act based on their perceptions of what they believe to be true, it is fundamental to the success of a collaborative change effort that we create a shared view of that truth. In a collaborative process, we are always asking the question: "What

do you mean by that word, phrase, or sentence?" to ensure a high degree of common understanding.

5. *An organizational culture has bottom-line value.* Most organizational problems are people-related, and therefore grounded in cultural differences. These differences and conflicts show up in the bottom line. It is critical to ensure that the core values of the company's culture are understood, accepted, and implemented.

Many of us talk about the company "culture," but the concept is usually considered to be either too "touchy-feely" or too amorphous to be of any bottom-line value to a company. What is a company culture? What difference does it make? The workplace culture represents the heart and soul of an organization—its values, beliefs, expectations, rituals, commitment, and attitudes of those who live in the work environment. In one sense, a workplace culture is the environment in which people choose to invest or not invest their energy, skills, and commitment. In another sense, a workplace culture represents the intangibles of a business—the informal organization; the pride its workers have in their work; their enthusiasm and energy level; their relationships with each other; and their commitment and loyalty to the goals of the enterprise— its vision. It is the passion, excitement, and enthusiasm that the members of the organization have for their work, their relationships with each other, and the vision. Still another way to think about the workplace culture is as that special something that differentiates one company from another.

Workplace cultures have the power to add significant value to the bottom line. When a workforce is not aligned on a common set of values, the business suffers. When workers do share the same basic set of values, their energy gets focused on producing bottom-line success for the company.

6. *Integrity begins at the top.* The integrity that any organization's leaders are perceived to have is based, to a great extent, on whether they "walk the talk." For example, an executive at a Fortune 500 company that had "valuing people" as part of its vision was quoted as saying during the company's downsizing effort that the workforce was "lucky to have a job" and should stop complaining about the lack of empowerment. The lack of congruence be-

tween the company vision and the actual behavior of the executive resulted in a loss of credibility and loyalty. The behavior of the workforce shifted from one of commitment to the company to one of anger, resentment, and fear about their personal economic survival—not an environment conducive to excellent results.

For any organization to be successful in an increasingly chaotic market, there must be a solid values foundation. Central to that foundation is the integrity its leaders and members exhibit. To transcend the culture war and achieve cultural reconciliation, there must be trust, credibility, and respect. To achieve this, the integrity of leadership must be above reproach.

Collaboration: A Framework for Peace in the Workplace

These working assumptions provide the cornerstone for the principle of *collaboration*, the new cultural framework that can replace hierarchy as the basis for how we lead, manage, and organize work. This principle not only honors these fundamental assumptions and our cultural heritage, but also recognizes the realities of what it takes to run a business. As a framework for leading and managing an organization, collaboration provides a common ground and a basis for mediating the profound value differences that presently exist in most organizations.

Ultimately, collaboration as an organizing principle is about authentic, honest relationships and their requirements: self-esteem, respect, integrity, responsibility, and alignment. In its application to work situations, collaboration provides the common denominator for engaging all members of the workforce. As a cultural framework for leading and managing an enterprise, collaboration is a work ethic that governs human behavior in the organization—across groups, teams, and even companies. The application of collaboration to the work environment, then, is what we will call the "Collaborative Work Ethic."

Figure 2-2. The seven core values of collaboration.

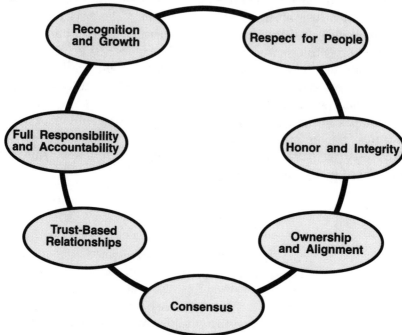

The Seven Core Values of
the Collaborative Work Ethic

The Collaborative Work Ethic is a group of seven core values that provide the foundation for the Collaborative Workplace. This crucial set of beliefs begin from the premise that people come first in the organization, that people produce results, and that to do so, they must be motivated at the level of the heart and spirit. This ethic recognizes that a high level of motivation is most likely to come when the workforce "owns" their workplace culture and when their objectives are aligned with the company's strategic direction. Results are thus achieved by creating a work environment grounded in a core set of values, using consensus-based processes to build that ownership and alignment. The seven core values that comprise the Collaborative Work Ethic are shown in Figure 2-2 and discussed in the following sections.

Value 1: *Respect for People*

The fundamental building block for any organization is individual self-esteem. In order for people to collaborate from a position of strength and equality, they need a high level of self-esteem and/or a work environment that actively seeks to enhance and support the building of self-esteem. Self-esteem is the positive sense of self reflected in an individual's authenticity, courage, integrity, trust, dignity, self-respect, and wholeness. Self-esteem is a person's sense of self-worth. In a collaborative work environment, positive self-esteem produces self-empowerment, and out of that personal empowerment comes the ability to empower others and build trust-based relationships.

A work culture that demonstrates respect for people understands that quality and service are created by people and by their attitudes toward work, the company, and their customers. It understands that people have value in their own right. Finally, a work culture that respects people understands the need for a long-range investment in their growth and development.

People feel valued when their work environment is nurturing and caring; when they are given room to grow, make mistakes, and learn; when they can operate in an environment free of fear; and when they feel assured of accountability, honest communication, compassion, and coaching. In such an environment, management shifts its role from one of authority, telling, controlling, and monitoring to one of facilitating, coaching, mentoring, and counseling; there is no "boss."

Value 2: *Honor and Integrity*

In many cultures, honor and integrity drive individual behavior. In Japan, for example, personal dishonor is considered so grave a misfortune that even today there are cases of hari-kari, or ritual suicide, in which people end their lives rather than go on living with their honor ruined. In our culture, integrity is central to an individual's sense of honor and self-respect. Put one way, I am my word, and if I do not keep my word, I am out of integrity. If I am out of integrity, I may dishonor my name and lose the trust, faith, and confidence of others. I may become known as someone who does not keep his word. To use Steven Covey's term, I am not trust-worthy.* In a Collaborative Workplace, honoring one's commitments and agreements is an essential building block in the success of the organization. Because people are interdependent, we need to trust each other, which means I must believe in others' integrity. In a collaborative work organization, it is also my responsibility to protect the integrity of the collaborative process and to uphold its values.

Value 3: Ownership and Alignment

People usually take care of what they own. As a colleague used to say, "No one ever washes a rented car." When the workforce has a true sense of ownership of the workplace, the job, and the enterprise, there is a greater likelihood they will take good care of it. When they feel alienated or not part of the business, their work becomes just a job, where they tend to operate on the principle of compliance. In a Collaborative Workplace, leadership proactively engages the workforce in building ownership of the organization. This process requires commitment from several types of people:

- *Leaders and managers* providing new opportunities for psychological ownership, creating team-based processes built on consensus, and allowing people to risk and grow.
- *Process owners* actively engaging the members of the organization in participating in decisions and even becoming process owners themselves.
- *Organization systems owners* redesigning their systems to encourage and reward more extensive interaction and collaboration.
- *Turf managers* giving up their perceived right to turf and playing by a new set of agreements that involve more horizontal and cross-functional interaction.

While it may seem to the current owners that they are giving up control, their ownership is really a myth. An organization is

*Steven R. Covey, *The Seven Habits of Highly Effective People* (New York: Simon & Schuster, 1989).

not like a piece of real estate. The true owners of the organization reside in its workplace. By increasing their stake in its success, the managers can do nothing but gain.

Equally important is the value of alignment that is driven by a high level of ownership. You can have an empowered organization but go out of business. So, if ownership is the rocket booster, alignment is the guidance system. The processes designed to achieve strategic alignment within the organization will enable the collaborative organization to hit its true market niche, serve its customers with excellence, and outstrip the competition.

In a more traditional sense, alignment occurs when all the members of an organization agree on the vision, mission, and strategic course of action for the company or organization. It also occurs when the company is aligned with the market, is demonstrating its unique and value-added role, and is focused on achieving competitive advantage.

Value 4: Consensus

It is generally accepted now that the most effective set of working relationships are those based on the idea of win-win, although there are many different interpretations of what win-win amounts to. In order for a win-win to occur, there must be a consensus on the decision, the outcome, and even the process for arriving at it. Otherwise, we are talking about compromise, "I can live with it," and other win-lose, or lose-lose arrangements.

Webster defines *consensus* as "group solidarity in sentiment and belief, unanimity; a judgment arrived at by most of those concerned." In a Collaborative Workplace 100 percent of the parties to the decision must fully agree in order to achieve a true win-win. This means that they must work through their disagreements to achieve a more powerful agreement. Another way of looking at consensus is that it is a decision-making rule in which every party to the decision *fully supports* the decision, sees value in the result, and will actively defend the decision.

Many people confuse consensus with compromise or "I can live with it"—as in "I can tolerate that decision." People who work in a can-live-with organizational culture tend to act out their differences outside the team or group, resulting in many disconnects and the erosion of trust in their relationships. True collaboration requires that individuals in a group responsible for an outcome work *through* their differences, building a new level of understanding and awareness of one another's legitimate concerns, creating a new level of synergy, and deriving the best solution for a given situation.

Value 5: Trust-Based Relationships

The leader of an information systems project team said it best: "It's not about technology or power anymore; it's about relationships." In the networked organization, authority no longer works as the basis for work relationships. Trust is the new glue. If you are in London, Jane is in New York, and I am in Chicago, we may have to reach consensus on a critical business decision by teleconference. In doing so, it is essential that we trust one another—know that we will honor our agreements and follow through on the decisions we reach.

Most people want trust and openness at work. They also want to *be* trusted. But trust does not come easily. In fact, most of us have little trust in each other, which feeds a host of organizational problems. Establishing trust in our work relationships is one of the first orders of business in any collaborative work environment. Of equal importance is maintaining trust by ensuring that the ups and downs of our work relationships are worked out face-to-face.

Trust takes time and begins with self-trust. In relationships, it is earned through careful nurturing, and it is maintained by ensuring the integrity of the relationship, which can even involve "tough love." Once broken, trust is sometimes never regained. In a collaborative work environment it can be regained through creating an opportunity for personal accountability and forgiveness. The building of trust-based relationships requires time, a supportive work environment, freedom from reprisals, and a significant level of interpersonal skill.

Value 6: Full Responsibility and Accountability

What does it mean to be fully responsible for the success of my team, my group, and my company? Does it mean I have to be my brother's keeper, monitor others' actions, and take corrective action? Does it mean I have authority? In the hierarchical paradigm, people are isolated from one another by their job descriptions, titles, and organizational units. Each person is responsible only for what is listed in his or her description. Managers are responsible for all the work done. Staff meetings and the individual use of authority are vehicles for coordination. Evaluations are techniques for ensuring that results are produced. Responsibility flows downward through delegation and the parceling out of authority. Accountability flows upward and is often punitive in intent or reality.

In the Collaborative Workplace, full responsibility is an individual act of commitment. In this environment, the individual takes on the *shared responsibility* for the success of the team, the group, and the company. It means that an individual deals directly with a team member if work is not being completed on schedule. *Direct dealings* are an essential tool as people learn how to support one another. It is a new level of responsibility that requires skill. It means moving beyond complaining and gossip to being part of the solution, recommending options, and taking action in collaboration with colleagues. If, for example, a member's well-being or work is negatively affected by outside family pressures, alcohol or drug abuse, or if his or her behavior is not supportive of the mission, each one of us is responsible for addressing the problem and bringing the issue to resolution. In the Collaborative Workplace, we do not wait for management to handle these problems.

Accountability, in the collaborative paradigm, is where the rubber hits the road. It is where we hold ourselves and one another to account in order to maintain the highest standards of behavior and performance. In many respects, it is not an act of authority, but one of faith and compassion. Ultimately, accountability is about our individual integrity and the reputation of our team and company.

True accountability as a value can only be fully achieved in an environment free of fear. We have to be able to take risks, make mistakes, learn, and grow. If every time I try to do something different or take a risk I get my hand slapped, get demeaned, or get devalued, I will not continue to risk, learn, or grow. At the same time, we have to find a way to hold each other accountable for what we do or do not do.

In the Collaborative Workplace, we have to reset the context for accountability. You can run, but you cannot hide. We are all accountable to one another. We cannot hide behind our rank, the data, or our expertise, because we know it takes us all to make it work. There are several levels of accountability:

- *Accountability as personal integrity.* I know when I have not done my job well or have failed to do it at all. It is my responsibility to be accountable to my team and tell them before they find out. It is my personal integrity that is on the line. I am also accountable for protecting the integrity of the collaborative process. When I am "out of integrity," I take responsibility for it, learn from it, and recommit to my values.

- *Accountability as direct dealings.* Whether I am found out or not, I owe it to my team, my committee, or my group to be proactive and to advise them of the issue, problem, or need and propose solutions. I should not wait until the problem is beyond solution, or until we have the next team meeting. I also owe it to a team member to deal directly with any behaviors, actions, or inactions I believe are detrimental to his or her well-being or value to the team or the company. This direct dealing may occur either off-line or, if not successful in the team or group, as part of the ongoing work process.

- *Accountability as coaching and counseling.* Should the individual not respond well to direct dealings, either off-line or in the group, the next step is to offer the individual one-on-one coaching from a respected senior member of the team. (Authority has nothing to do with this level of support, although the two may be synonymous.) If coaching does not work, then a higher level of intervention in the form of counseling, both professional and/or psychological, may be necessary.

- *Accountability as administrative action.* In the Collaborative Workplace we do not shy away from corrective action when it is found necessary. It is the court of last, not first, resort and should be used sparingly. It may be necessary to remove an individual from the work environment. The success of the Collaborative

Workplace is most likely to occur when we can move away from the view of responsibility and accountability as being a policing function grounded in a top-down approach to relationships. Instead, we must move toward a view that full responsibility and accountability are horizontal, shared, and grounded in our individual and collective integrity as adults and professionals.

Value 7: Recognition and Growth

Perhaps one of the most difficult work environments is one in which "one mistake is worth 100 attaboys." In a constantly changing work environment, it needs to be okay for people to make some mistakes, to take risks, to try new things, and to learn and grow. We cannot be competitive without risk, and it is not possible to risk without making mistakes.

Human beings respond best to rewards and recognition and learn best in an environment free from fear. That does not mean to say that such an environment is free of accountability, as just discussed. It is important to create a way to celebrate one another, to move beyond awards with little meaning to a truly genuine and institutionalized process of recognition for contributions beyond completion of tasks, but also for service to others. We might recognize innovation, creativity, team effort, or customer service. The point in a Collaborative Workplace is to encourage ongoing, instantaneous recognition of one another by all members of the team or group. Recognition should not be a top-down prerogative, nor should it only happen once a year. What is also important is that the rewards and recognition process be internally consistent, that it reward the values expected in the work environment. In addition, the application of this value may result in the entire rewards and recognition process being redesigned to support individual, team, and company performance.

A second aspect of this principle is the importance of learning and growing as an integral part of the collaborative process. As part of the project cycle, for example, there should be a debriefing on every aspect of a project for lessons learned—both positive and negative—and any suggested improvements should be integrated and institutionalized in the next project cycle. But this approach to continuous improvement also applies to group and individual learning. The focus must be on process skills and cultural adjustments as well as on bottom-line systems or structural changes. This level of learning and growing can also result in substantive changes in the career development processes in the business.

In addition, a growing environment can be committed to what we will call "self-renewal." Nothing is stagnant. Organizations may want to commit to constant self-renewal and constant questioning of their assumptions. They may be open to the possibility that they have anomalies that cannot be explained away by their current paradigm. Self-renewal, in this sense, is a process that ensures that the company will remain flexible, proactive, and able to shift to new paradigms as they emerge.

Conclusion

In an age when the social contract has often been broken—when millions of people have been laid off, when hierarchy is less effective, when cultural warfare continues unabated—we need a cultural framework that brings peace to the workplace. We need a firm foundation that gives us stability in the face of unrelenting change and integrity in the face of broken contracts. The core values of the Collaborative Workplace allow us to do just that, shifting the paradigm by allowing us to take responsibility for the transformation.

3

Creating the Collaborative Culture

You get the behavior you tolerate.
—Plato

At Dynap Corporation, things had always been that way, and no one said anything about it. Most people would not talk about it; they just lived with it. The vice president for production had consistently pitted one member of the staff against another, often giving several of his direct reports the same assignment. When the results were not to his liking, he would single out the individuals by name at staff meetings and critique their work, often seriously embarrassing them. His organization was not a place that encouraged questions or challenges to management's direction.

It did not take long for new employees to realize that if they wanted to advance their careers they had to deal directly with the vice president. It was not uncommon to see people lined up outside his office at 7:30 in the morning to get their issues handled. Power and influence were the name of the game. "Every man for himself" was the rule. Trust was something to be developed outside the workplace or in the hidden culture.

Respect, trust, and honesty are three of the most important ingredients in achieving competitive advantage in an increasingly chaotic marketplace. The management style of command-and-control, which uses power to create a culture of fear, produces predictable behavioral results. The workforce will comply with the stated and unstated rules of the road, but their productivity, energy, and loyalty to the company will suffer.

What does it take to create a workplace culture in which respect, trust, and honesty are the norm rather than the exception? How do we create a work environment in which people are willing to take responsibility for the success of the enterprise and be held accountable for their results? How can we begin to change from old cultures and behaviors to a work environment that will work for us rather than against us?

This chapter looks first at the requirements for creating the collaborative culture where trust can grow. It then defines a specific governance process called Operating Agreements that will result in the realignment of the organization's culture and work relationships to the Collaborative Work Ethic. Finally, the chapter examines in detail the 15 Operating Agreements needed by most teams, groups, and organizations for their collaborative culture to work.

Creating a Responsible Work Environment

To paraphrase Plato, we get the behavior or culture we create. If the workforce at Dynap did not like to operate in fear, whose responsibility was it to change the situation? Every organization's culture is governed by a psychological contract or covenant, a set of mutually agreed to understandings or accepted values about how we will work together. In the conventional covenant of command-and-control, those understandings or values are only tacitly agreed to by the workforce. They are not explicitly discussed or consented to. People are expected either to know them or to figure them out. In the creation of a new covenant, however, people can openly discuss and consent to a new set of agreements that will allow them to produce respect, trust, and honesty in their work relationships. There are several requirements necessary for creating this new culture:

- *Principle-based agreements.* In many organizations, the covenant is based on power or the preferences of one person. In a collaborative culture, the first requirement is that all agreements be based on principle. Specifically, the core values of the Collaborative Work Ethic (as discussed in Chapter 2) provide a framework for teams, groups, and companies to clarify how their members choose to work together.

- *An explicit governance process.* The second requirement is that the process be explicit and not secret. The rules that govern most work environments are usually unspoken (e.g., "I won't step on you if you won't step on me"; "No surprises"; or "Don't shoot the messenger"). In one company, there was even an unspoken understanding that "No good deed goes unpunished." In creating a collaborative culture, the unspoken rules are made explicit and agreed to by all parties. In a collaborative culture there are no secrets or hidden agendas. This way, people know what is expected of them; they have bought into the agreements and take responsibility for their full implementation.

- *A behavioral shift.* The third requirement is that everyone engage in a significant shift in behavior—both as individuals and as a team, group, or organization. It is not easy to give up the tried and true processes we used in a power-based culture. Since those values and processes hurt our competitive position, we are each challenged to change our behavior. As Figure 3–1 shows, the process of creating a Collaborative Workplace means a gradual movement away from behaviors characterized by avoidance, accommodation, competition, or compromise to behaviors based on true collaboration.

- *Operating agreements.* The fourth requirement is that we establish the behavioral rules to govern how we will work together, through what we will call "Operating Agreements." Operating Agreements *become* the collaborative culture because they represent the values and beliefs of the members of the team, group, or company. The process of creating these agreements brings the key values and beliefs of the participants to the surface, and when tied to the core values of the Collaborative Work Ethic, redefines the work culture that can transform the organization and result in the needed behavioral shift. As members take responsibility for their behavior, they become accountable to one another and responsible for the success of their organization. Operating Agreements appear to be a simple concept, but the process requires that each individual examine his or her own behavior and values and choose to adjust them in a way that supports the new culture.

Figure 3–1. The behavioral shift.

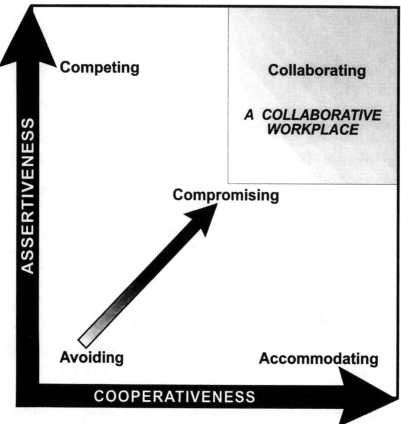

A Definition of Operating Agreements

In a collaborative governance process, Operating Agreements are defined as:

The principle-based agreements we have with each other that provide the foundation for respectful, honest, and trust-based relationships and teamwork.

Put another way, Operating Agreements are how we will behave and work together to create a work environment of respect, trust, and honesty. Operating Agreements are the collective conscience, the consensus culture that enables any organization to transform itself and become a more stable, civil, and productive workplace.

Three distinctions are important here. First, *Operating Agreements are not "ground rules."* Almost every team, group, or organization has a set of tactical rules in place to ensure that meetings start on time and end on time and that members respect one another's opinions. In the Operating Agreements process, however, the workforce is engaged in a profound conversation about their basic values and beliefs concerning how work should be done, how decisions should be made, how disagreements should be resolved, and how accountability should be ensured.

Second, *Operating Agreements are a form of prevention.* Operating Agreements cover a team's basic behavioral requirements. These agreements are made up-front in the process of forming the team. They become a significant way to prevent conflicts down the road, since everyone knows how they will be handled. Operating Agreements arm the members of a team or group with the tools they need to be self-sufficient in working through their differences, speed up work processes, and leverage the synergies of the group.

Third, *Operating Agreements become the new workplace culture.* As a process, they ensure cultural and behavioral alignment among team members. They represent the shared view of all team members on what they believe to be important about their behavior. They are the cornerstone of the collaborative governance process and provide the basis for the empowerment and accountability of any type of team.

The 15 Core Operating Agreements

To be successful, most teams, groups, and organizations need to establish 15 core Operating Agreements. (See Figure 3–2.) In the balance of this chapter, each of these agreements will be discussed and key points and distinctions for consideration identified. (A sample team's Operating Agreements may be found in Appendix I.)

Figure 3–2. A team's Operating Agreements.

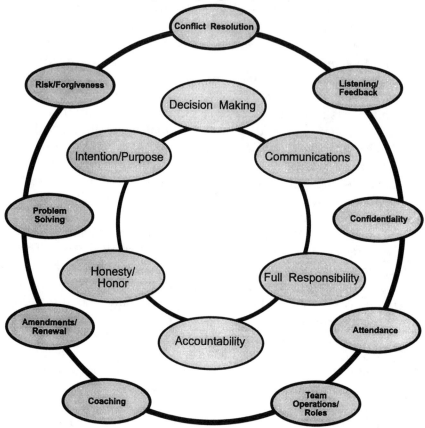

Agreement 1: Decision Making

This is the first and certainly the most difficult agreement any team or group consents to. It lies at the heart of the team's operations and opens a window on the team's soul, providing an indicator of how it will treat the rest of the Operating Agreements process. What we have learned from teams is that as this initial agreement unfolds, other agreements are suggested. For example, when a team concludes that it wants consensus as its decision-making rule on strategic issues, it may become important to address the Attendance Agreement. It is valuable to identify these other agreements as you go along, but try to stay focused on the topic at hand.

The Decision-Making Agreement, however, is not about agreement; it is about disagreement and how team members choose to handle their difference with one another. Let's look at a number of key distinctions that must be made.

The Decision-Making Options

Every group process has a decision-making rule. There are really just four options to choose from:

1. Decision making by one person
2. Minority rule (less than 50 percent but more than one person)
3. Majority rule (less than 100 percent but more than 50 percent
4. Consensus (100 percent)

In the beginning, most groups base this process on experience with majority rule and the use of *Robert's Rules of Order* as a guide. Most groups also say initially that they are comfortable with *compromise* or *can live with* as the basis for how their decision will be made. But when pressed, they usually choose *consensus*, because very few people really want to be left out of decisions that will affect them. This, then, leads to a much more difficult distinction.

Our Lack of Experience With Consensus

We need look no further than celebrity murder trials to know that juries do not work by true consensus, even though this is the one place where we believe 100 percent is the rule. The press stories of juries are replete with examples of the browbeating, intimidation, guilt, and fear that drive dissenting jurors to relent and cave in to peer pressure. The only other place in our culture where consensus is institutionalized as a decision-making rule is in the Quaker Meeting, in which consensus is required. Everywhere else our decisions are made by one person, by a minority, or by a majority. We do not have a lot of experience with consensus—even though that is how most people would like to operate. Lacking this experience, we tend to rely on processes we are familiar with: compromise and cooperation.

Consensus vs. Compromise

When asked to define *consensus,* someone on the team is likely to say it means "Can live with it," as in, "I can live with that decision." In effect, this means that I will compromise my true feelings on the issue because I want to get along, or because I do not have the technical expertise, or because it does not really matter to me. I will certainly argue my point of view, but when all is said and done, I will go along with the group. This approach to consensus means I may not really have to take responsibility for the decision; I can always opt out and shift that responsibility to someone else who "knows more about it." It also means I may choose whether or not I want to fully participate in the discussion. I have given myself a trapdoor. The "can live with" philosophy represents a win-lose approach to decision making because, in a compromise, someone always loses something. In effect, rather than face their differences, these individuals avoid the issue. Then, when the going gets tough, they can turn around and say to the team, "I told you so." The bottom line is that compromise does not equal consensus!

One management team we worked with became very creative in adopting what it called a "supermajority" rule: that is, all but one person on the team had to agree. What this meant was that one member could disagree, but the team would not be obligated to work through the disagreement. This type of trapdoor meant that the true synergies of the team could not be tapped, because often they lay in the very perspectives that the one person disagreeing could offer. The team's trapdoor only succeeded in trapping it into not taking full responsibility.

The Power of True Consensus

True consensus occurs when there is no member of the team or group who has any reservations *whatsoever* about the decision that has been reached. The "whatsoever" is critical. This means no trapdoors, no "I can live with it," no smoke screens, no windows still open for dissent: The architecture of disagreement has disappeared. With true consensus, we become genuinely aligned and have ownership of the decisions we have made. Because I know you will keep your agreements, my trust in you goes up, and I won't need to spend time protecting my flank; I can focus on real work and on the customer instead.

One way of knowing when there is true consensus is that the level of energy in the group goes up, even when everyone is tired after a long day's work. At a more profound level, in a constantly changing work environment, we know consensus is at work when the workplace culture does not change even though the structure or work processes do.

Focusing Consensus Decisions

With the trapdoors sealed, teams often start to differentiate among the types of decisions an organization or group needs to make using consensus. Some decisions will be considered strategic or policy-oriented, impacting the direction of the business. Other decisions will be considered tactical, having to do with implementing the overall strategies, while still others will be classified as operational, or day-to-day, decisions. These terms mean different things to each of us, since one person's floor is another's ceiling. So it is critical to define and clarify what we mean. As the team works through these distinctions, it will tend to use consensus for its strategic decisions.

When Disagreements Arise

Most of us avoid conflicts, either because we don't like to, want to, or know how to disagree. So we enter this process with resistance and avoidance as our starting points. As one team member expressed it, "Disagreement makes me vulnerable. I do not know how it will turn out, whether there will be anger, and what price I will have to pay. It makes me afraid." Fear becomes the driver in keeping us from an honest exchange of differing views. Additional reluctance to disagree comes from not knowing how to disagree in a constructive way that enhances the work relationship. In effect, we are amateurs in human dynamics who are trying to become trained acrobats without a safety net beneath us.

What we absolutely must do together is develop a safety net, a known process by which we can disagree, be respected, and not fear repudiation, the silent treatment, intimidation, or reprisal. We can do this by explicitly agreeing that dissent is welcome, even expected in our team.

Opening the Dissent Window

In a manufacturing company's information systems group, the members had nearly reached a consensus. All but two people were in agreement, yet these two persisted and persisted. The team went through all its processes and tools, but still it disagreed. What was the team going to do? No one knew the answer.

Teams need a tool to get to the bottom of their disagreements. In a Collaborative Workplace, this tool is called a *dissent window* and involves throwing open the "window of disagreement" to really listen to what their colleagues are concerned about. In using this tool, there is an obligation to hear what is actually being said, rather than what one wants to hear. This is very difficult to do, particularly when the pressure is on to make a timely decision. If anyone "runs over" the dissenter, however—by ridiculing or will-fully misinterpreting his or her arguments—the credibility and integrity of the whole team suffers. If it is worked out, mutual respect, trust, confidence, and honesty are the results.

From Smoke Screens to Safety Nets

Most teams will try the rational, intellectual approach to resolving differences; they will identify all the areas about which they agree, pinpoint where they don't, and begin to negotiate their way through the differences. Say there is a team member who continues to object to two key points and is unwilling to budge from this position. What is really going on? It may not be rational at all. It may be in the emotional realm. Sometimes people throw up smoke screens or introduce unrelated issues to avoid revealing what is really bothering them. Sometimes they do not even know why they are objecting; they just cannot agree. Team members have a responsibility to create a safety net for the disagreement— i.e., to work with the member to dissipate the smoke, get to the root cause, and help him or her move beyond the initial objections. When all the smoke has cleared, however, it is likely that the disagreement was about a significant emotional event in that person's past.

In a technology applications team, there were two members who expressed widely differing opinions on whether the new software application should be purchased. The debate went on for two hours. When the root-cause safety net was applied, it was discovered that one of the adversaries had lost a promotion and a significant pay increase in another organization because he had made a similar decision. Once this was uncovered, the team had new insights into the purchasing decision, and in five minutes was able to arrive at a much better decision.

Why Silence Is Not Golden

The price of admission is participation. In a collaborative team, verbal participation is a clear expectation. Sometimes individuals do not want to participate and are silent either because they are shy or upset, because they habitually avoid conflict, or because they just do not care. If members are going to be fully responsible for the success of the team, it is critical that everyone weigh in verbally. Silence is also not agreement. When it comes time to determine if there is a true consensus on a decision, it is important that there be some specific physical or verbal cue that every member uses to indicate positive or negative support. It is also important that everyone individually be given an opportunity to indicate his or her views. Silent members, or those hanging back, need to be directly engaged in the process. Failure to do so merely detracts from the effectiveness of the team down the road.

Agreement 2: Attendance

At a retail products company, the cross-functional team simply could not reach an agreement on how many of its members would attend any given meeting. In fact, the argument reached the point where it could not agree on whether to come to meetings on time or to stay for the duration. Clearly something else was going on.

Attendance at meetings can be a serious problem for teams, particularly when they have a consensus decision-making agreement that requires them to be present. Attendance can become a trapdoor. If the team is fighting over whether to be on time to meetings, a far more serious examination of underlying resistances is needed. What becomes critical, then, is how the team decides to set its priorities, handle its scheduling, and manage its time.

A related issue for a Collaborative Workplace is team gridlock. This can happen when there are so many teams operating by consensus that the schedules jam up because of crossover membership. It is important that the organization as a whole not over-assign individuals to various teams and that the teams be judicious in planning the number and frequency of their meetings.

Agreement 3: Intention and Purpose

Even with the best Operating Agreements, a team can get into trouble. One leadership team that had a complete list of agreements faced an ethical issue in which one member began to challenge the honesty of another. The argument became more and more heated until the team decided to reflect on what its intention was. Its Intention/Purpose Agreement was to "create a win-win and celebrate each other's success." With that agreement in mind, it decided to take the argument off-line and resolve it through third-party consultation. When it debriefed the experience later, it realized that without the Intention Agreement, the team might not have survived.

The dictionary defines *intention* as "that which [one] proposes to accomplish or attain; enduring the struggle and hardship; purpose or determination." Sooner or later, every team runs into a situation in which the other Operating Agreements simply do not work. Rational analysis does not work. Productivity is down, morale is lagging, and team spirit is at risk. What may be missing is clarity about the team's higher purpose, its reason for being that is more than just the content of its task or mission. In this sense, the

Intention/Purpose Agreement allows members of the organization to transcend the old paradigm, to break through their own self-imposed limitations to achieve fundamental group success.

Intention is the statement of the team's profound belief in itself.

Agreement 4: Full Responsibility

Jimmy, the company's night shift operator, had just finished his third 18-hour day in a row, and as he left, he forgot to close the drainage valve on the sludge pipe at the plant. The day's toxic waste ran off into the sound, killing 50,000 fish and creating a public relations nightmare for the company. The next day, when he reported to his team, he learned of the disaster. His colleagues were understandably furious with him for his incompetence. He had ruined a one-year safety track record, jeopardized their bonus pay, and embarrassed them all. Who was responsible? The team blamed Jimmy. Jimmy blamed management for making him work so many hours without a break. The town blamed the company. Management blamed the team and Jimmy. So who was truly responsible?

In the Collaborative Workplace each member of the team is fully responsible for the success of the team and the company. Failure at this level of magnitude means that everyone was responsible. We are our brother's keeper, whether we like it or not. It does not help to blame anyone.

Rather than blame—which produces all kinds of destructive behavior—why not problem-solve? Why not shift the paradigm? We can only do so in an environment that permits and even rewards risk taking, innovation, and creative solutions to problems. When a mistake is made, the team surrounds the person who made it, supports him or her, and looks for ways to avoid similar mistakes in the future.

Full responsibility also means that we have an obligation to each other—to take care of, support, and to watch out for one anothers' best interests. If a collegue we know who does not usually drink begins to stay out late and drink, do we not have a responsibility to say something? Or should we simply shrug and say, "Oh, that's not my business"? Where do we draw the line? Shouldn't someone have talked with management about the hours Jimmy was working and offered another solution, for example?

We cannot be fully empowered until we are willing to be fully responsible—to break through our self-imposed assumptions about how work is supposed to get done and take on all aspects of the job and the company's success. This means there is moral authority in our work relationships. It means learning to count on and be honest and forthright with each other. It means coaching and counseling one another, providing backup, and even moving to predictive maintenance of our work relationships—anticipating what might happen and putting preventive measures in place to avoid accidents and misunderstandings.

Agreement 5: Communication

We know good communication is critical to the success of our organizations. But what does that really mean, particularly in a Collaborative Workplace? We can think about communication more narrowly as a process or a set of tools. We can also think about it more broadly as a commitment to share full information to ensure full commitment.

"Mystery House" or Open House?

People need information to make decisions and do their work. In the absence of adequate or accurate information, they still have to make decisions, so they will "make it up." We call this the *mystery house*. In an organization where information is distributed only on a "need to know" or "ought to know" basis, there will be key people, many on the front line, who do not know about what is going on. In a rapidly changing business environment, this lack of information can only reduce the company's overall effectiveness.

The Communications Agreement can create an *open house*, a commitment to full and free-flowing information on a "want to know" basis. The agreement will spell out up-front who will get what information with what frequency and about what.

E-Mail and Voice-Mail

The Communications Agreement can also consider how members will communicate with each other. For example, some organizations are still paper-based and formally communicate through memos. When should memos be sent and when should the conversation be face-to-face? Many companies are using electronic- or voice-mail or computer-based groupware. Networked, global organizations cannot get their people face-to-face as often as they would like. But how do we use these media? For example, it is not advisable to use either E-mail or voice-mail to resolve an interpersonal dispute. Both types of communications are great, however, for keeping people updated and making logistical arrangements.

Careful attention should also be given to the use of teleconferences and video conferences—when to use them, how to engage the participants not in the meeting room, and how to follow through to ensure that the results have been bought into. I remember a video conference in which participants in the two outlying cities hit the mute button and later admitted they did so because they felt excluded from the mainstream conversation.

External Communication

A leadership team responsible for a major change process was holed up in conference rooms for the better part of three months with a tight lid on the proceedings to promote frankness and honesty. People in the organization, tired of being kept in the dark, began to circulate rumors about what was going on in the team. This put pressure on the team to engage the membership before it was ready. What should it say to the members? What should it tell its bosses? How should it handle its internal differences outside the room? What should its message be?

In effect, every team has its own public relations function that needs to be discussed, both up-front and as part of its regular meetings process. It is usually helpful to have an agreed-upon message that will be carried out of the meeting. It is better to have some information going out than none at all. This way the team itself is aligned and suspicions about its work are reduced.

Agreement 6: Confidentiality

Teams need to decide where to place the veil of privacy around their internal proceedings. If everything is kept confidential, others will wonder. If the dirty laundry is aired, the credibility of the team and the integrity of its processes may suffer significantly. The team has to achieve a balance appropriate to its specific circumstances. Usually teams make a decision not to report any personal opinions, differences, or conflicts that members have inside the team. Some even get more protective and refuse to report anything that will hurt the team or make it look bad.

In cross-functional teams whose members still report to their unit or division bosses, there is enormous pressure to tell all—particularly since performance reviews are done by that boss. To whom should the member be loyal—him- or herself, the boss, or the team? Here the integrity of the individual and the manager's commitment to the process are both tested. Will the boss trust the direct report to do what is best for the company? This must be sorted out both in the team and between the boss and the team member.

Agreement 7: Listening and Feedback

People often listen for what they want to hear—not to what is actually being said. We each have filters that screen out information that is dissonant with our worldview, beliefs, or way we think a situation should be handled. The Listening Agreement emphasizes the critical importance of what Steven Covey calls "empathic listening," in which we listen with our eyes.*

In the Collaborative Workplace, we also try to listen for what is behind what people say. "People," my office mate once told me, "never mean what they say. You have to figure out what they are really trying to tell you, and then respond to that message." By listening with our eyes—observing nonverbal behavior—and truly trying to understand what is being said, we open up a new channel for people to begin being truly honest.

---

*Steven R. Covey, *The Seven Habits of Highly Effective People* (New York: Simon & Schuster, 1989).

Feedback as Verbal Videotape

Giving and receiving feedback is equally difficult. We may not want to be honest about how we really feel about someone and risk the relationship. In giving feedback, our intent may be misinterpreted. So the safest way to operate is to not provide any feedback at all. As my mother used to say: "If you can't say something nice, don't say anything at all." Similarly, receiving individual feedback that is honest, authentic, and caring is difficult because it will most likely challenge one's beliefs and assumptions about oneself. As an executive recently told me, "It was not until I saw myself on videotape, giving a talk, that I truly realized that my beliefs about how I look and behave were simply not true." In creating the feedback part of this agreement, the team can choose how it will handle this process. Some additional skills training can also be helpful. Team members also need to learn to give and receive feedback in order to grow. If we keep quiet about things that are hurting the person or the team, the entire team suffers.

Agreement 8: Honesty and Honor

"Seek the truth and the truth shall set you free" is a common refrain. But we also know that telling the truth can sometimes get you fired. I am reminded of the senior vice president of a Fortune 100 company who once asked one of his direct reports after a meeting to be "honest" with him about his behavior. "Please," he said, "I need to know how I come across. I want to change my behavior. I need your help." So she told him. It was the last meeting they ever had.

We learn early on to not tell the truth. In fact there are many shades of truth telling, from "telling the truth, the whole truth, and nothing but the truth," to "white lies," to serious statements made by high public officials that are denied as "misstatements" the next day. We have even institutionalized the notion that the truth is what is expedient, and have found ourselves in situations in which we try to negotiate the truth in order to protect ourselves, our employees, our teams, or our organizations. The truth is usually already known in the organization. It just takes time for everyone to admit it. For our own honor and integrity, we have an obligation to tell the truth, particularly if we expect to build trust-based relationships. The Honesty and Honor Agreement can become very revealing. How do we know when someone is not telling the truth? Who are we to judge? Is this groupthink?

As a society and in business we sometimes let discussions of honesty and honor slip from the radar screen. The topic is very much alive in our everyday actions and practices. We need to keep it high on the agenda of conscious discussion, no matter how uncomfortable it is. In coming to terms with our different perceptions of the truth, we raise the level of discourse, come truly to a level of principle, and increase the prospects that we may behave with honor and dignity, not only as individuals but also as teams, groups, and organizations.

Agreement 9: Problem Solving

When a team tackles problems, it needs to distinguish between a content and process problem. We usually interpret problems in terms of the task we have to accomplish. They have a content component. But just as many—if not more—problems involve interpersonal and behavioral issues. As a consequence of our bias in favor of content, teams may find themselves in rational-analytic discussions about things that have little or no relevance to the real problem. Problems are multifaceted and need to be treated as such. They require process consciousness and a willingness to address the realities of these issues.

No solution can be better than the definition of the problem. We need to invest up-front time in problem definition. The Problem-Solving Agreement needs to create a process that enables teams to look for "true North"—i.e., to get as close to defining the real problem as possible. This means that we must dispense with our usual interpretations and get to root causes. NASA learned early on that the best answers to complex problems were found through the synergy of the team. Engaging the full team provides a system of checks and balances that prevents any single individual's interpretations of reality from dominating the process.

Agreement 10: Conflict Resolution

In the Dynap Corporation, a major marketing organization was located 100 miles from the product development group. From a business standpoint, each needed the other to give full service to their clients. Two individuals, one in each group, had had a falling out eight years before. They never talked about it, let alone resolved it. Within a short period both groups had become focused on their side's being right. The conflict appeared irreconcilable. But did it matter who was right? Where was the customer in all this?

How often have we heard the expression "Never go to bed mad"? In business, we would do well to operate by a similar maxim: "Never leave work mad." In organizations where people do not resolve their conflicts, there is a tendency to hold on to bad feelings, to list the points at issue in mental "dossiers" on Fred, Carol, and Richard, and to collect corroborating evidence. Conflicts become grudges, "votes" are collected on the character of certain individuals, and informal networks are used to isolate those individuals. A grudge can become a vendetta, and what was once just a small issue can become an insurmountable barrier.

Conflict Resolution

If the Israelis and Palestinians can sit down together and talk peace, then any conflict at work can be resolved. The real question is—do we *want* to resolve it? We have to genuinely want to end a conflict before it can be resolved. It is helpful to know that every conflict has a life cycle. As Figure 3–3 suggests, there is usually a "presenting situation," that can escalate into a significant difference. If the difference cannot be effectively addressed early on, the escalation process continues. But when you are ready to leave the room, is when you *must* stay—knowing that the crisis will pass and that often people just need to be truly heard, to vent their feelings, and to get the anger out. That is when you can you make the intervention to begin resolving the differences.

Being Right vs. Being in Relationship

The cost of being right all the time is that we lose our connection with the other person. What does that prove? What difference does it make? Maybe he or she is wrong. Maybe we just have a different interpretation of what happened and that is where the cause of the conflict lies.

In a high-level information systems team, Sarah refused to sit

Figure 3–3. The conflict cycle.

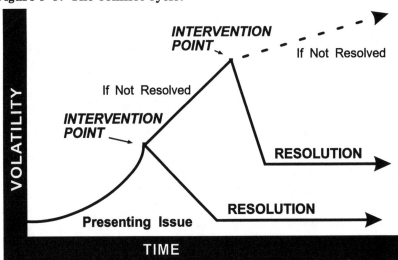

across the table from or next to Marilyn. It got rather awkward, since there were only nine people on the team. After two days of working through their Operating Agreements, the two sat down over drinks after dinner and talked long into the night. They discovered that Sarah had thought Marilyn was responsible for her demotion three years ago, while Marilyn had thought Sarah was a rude, angry person. Sarah did not know that Marilyn had absented herself from the performance review because of a conflict of interest. They were both right, but not in relationship with each other. From that moment on the trust built and their organizations began to work closely together. They realized what a waste of time and energy the three years of misunderstanding had been.

Direct Dealings as the Key to Success

The CEO did not like the use of his company's trademark by his strategic alliance partner, so he asked his legal department to "handle it." But when the other company's general counsel received the formal letter about using the trademark, he hit the roof. The legal missiles were exchanged, and the alliance nearly came to a standstill until top management at both companies sat down in private to resolve the dispute. Significant damage to mutual trust, however, had been done. Why hadn't the CEO simply made a telephone call or dealt directly with the other executive? Fear? Discomfort? It is amazing how many of our business relationship issues could be resolved easily if we only took the trouble to sit down and talk face-to-face about our concerns. Better yet, we could have an agreement to deal directly with each other on all conflicts.

A variation on this theme is called "triangulation"—talking to a third party about a complaint instead of talking directly to the individual. Within hours the informal network, or gossip, has rendered a judgment about that individual's character. Direct dealings solve this problem.

The Importance of Timing

We also tend to let our conflicts simmer, as in the marketing example previously discussed. When garbage is left to rot on the sidewalk during a sanitation strike, the possibility of disease increases daily. In business, we are often willing, for various reasons, to let our conflicts remain unresolved for days, weeks, even years. The rule of thumb here is to have an agreement to address conflicts as close to the event as possible.

Agreement 11: Risk/Forgiveness

It took Thomas Edison 10,000 mistakes to invent the lightbulb. At the risk of having to be forgiven for quoting an icon of early childhood education, Big Bird of Sesame Street fame has a song that starts with the line: "Everyone makes mistakes, oh yes they do." *Me,* make mistakes? You've got to be kidding! We think we cannot afford to make mistakes, so we put the brakes on all risk-taking behavior. But without risk, we cannot be fully entrepreneurial and innovative, and we lose competitive advantage.

Asking for Forgiveness, Not Permission

For middle managers in particular, there is not a lot of room to make mistakes in an economic environment where we must do more with less. In an environment of fear, it is not likely we will risk making a mistake, becoming visible, and having the incident become a serious career event. One way management is dealing with the risk issue is to say: "It's easier to ask for forgiveness than for permission." This speaks to the deep level of frustration felt by many managers about corporate bureaucracy and the sense that, since the answer will probably be no if they ask for permission, it's better *not* to ask.

The paradox is that to achieve competitive advantage, we must risk, make mistakes, and learn. No pain, no gain. We need to be willing to lose what we have in order to achieve competitive advantage. To do that we need to create a workplace culture in which people will eagerly risk, innovate, and create. This means that management, owners, and shareholders might consider looking more at the long-term results of the business and encouraging their members to risk. Risking behavior can even be rewarded, as long as it is understood that people must learn from any mistakes they make.

Creating a Learning Environment

Most of us need permission to admit we do not know it all, that we do make mistakes. The paradigm shift in the Collaborative Workplace is to move toward a work environment in which the workforce feels psychologically safe—in which fear and compliance are replaced by mutual support and learning. In the Risk/ Forgiveness Agreement, the team needs to consider creating a process called *blanket amnesty* in which individuals are encouraged to come up with new ideas and acknowledge mistakes—with the team members actively considering new and innovative ways to learn and grow the company from those experiences. These lessons are then documented and periodically reviewed to ensure that they are codified. Then, every two years, except for matters of health and safety, the team throws the code away and starts all over again.

Agreement 12: Team Operations/Roles

With leadership in a collaborative team being a function rather than a position, the team may experience a significant disconnect for a while about how to do specific jobs that the "leader" used to perform. We will talk about these various roles in Chapter 4, but it is important to mention here that the tasks of managing a team and its day-to-day operations still needs to be performed. In the Team/Operations Agreement, the team sorts out how these responsibilities will be handled and by whom. The role of the "contact" person is particularly useful in that he or she can take on the logistical meeting design and facilitation functions for a period of, say, three to six months, and then the position can be rotated. This process increases the level of capability and self-confidence among all members as each takes turn handling one of the most critical jobs in any collaborative team.

Agreement 13: Coaching

Many people think of coaching strictly in terms of sports. The coach is someone who tells us where we went wrong, encourages us to do our personal best, and gives the plays to the leader. In the Collaborative Workplace, coaching takes on a very different flavor. First, coaching, like leadership, is a function, not a position, and like the other leadership responsibilities of the authority-based leader, the coaching role needs to be shifted to the team. Second, each member at the same time becomes a coach in the sense of providing mutual support and becoming fully responsible and accountable for the success of the team and company. Third, coaching is an obligation based on mutual respect, which we take seriously, always looking for enhancements in our productivity and effectiveness.

The Coaching Agreement spells out the process by which the coaching function will be shared. The process agreed to will probably incorporate or overlay many other agreements already reached, such as the Listening and Feedback Agreement. Addressing the issue of how they will apportion the responsibilities of the coaching role will help the team members sort out how they will achieve some degree of equality.

Agreement 14: Accountability

In a hierarchical organization, being held accountable is usually a negative experience and something to be feared. It involves having to defend, CYA, or provide rational arguments for actions. People often hide behind paper, process, or position to avoid being held accountable. But in the Collaborative Workplace they realize that they do not need to hide. They can look forward to opportunities to engage their colleagues in an honest conversation about how a goal was or was not accomplished and how it can be done better.

In the Collaborative Workplace, each team member takes full responsibility for the success of the organization. It is a place where we can make mistakes and learn. Accountability is something I choose to do myself, without having to hide or fear being caught. In Chapter 2, we discussed the specific ways in which members can hold themselves and others accountable through personal integrity; direct dealings, coaching and counseling; and administrative action. Just because people are committed to holding themselves and others accountable, however, does not mean that it will automatically happen. There are consequences. What might they be?

At the Business Level

When a workforce chooses to begin operating collaboratively, it cannot forget its business obligation to produce on the bottom line. Peoples Express had a very empowered workforce, but it went out of business. There are consequences in every organization for the failure to perform and meet the needs of the market, the customers, and the shareholders. In a Collaborative Workplace, we use a tough test for accountability in the marketplace: the strategic alignment method (to be discussed in Chapter 5). This method engages the entire organization in a collaborative process that results in a clear determination of the business' unique and value-added role and competitive advantage in the market, and that ensures that all key stakeholders are aligned around and own its strategic direction. Effective alignment will mean that the members of the organization will learn from its mistakes, take responsibility for the success of the business, and determine together the most appropriate course of action. This process does not abrogate the traditional role of leadership. Rather, it enhances and empowers the new leadership function.

Figure 3–4. Empowerment and accountability.

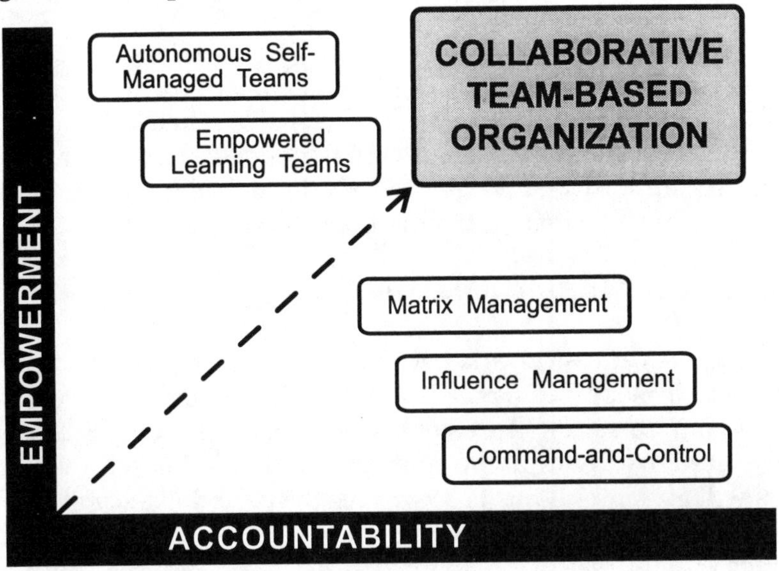

At the Team Level

Many individuals and teams have overreacted to the idea of empowerment and confused it with autonomous action. After years of being told what to do, the opportunity to do what the team thinks is right, in spite of management, is almost too good to pass up. But allowing the pendulum to swing too far one way or the other misses the point. As Figure 3–4 suggests, we must have *empowerment with accountability.* This is achieved not only by the strategic alignment method, but also by the Operating Agreements process, which ensures a commitment to team accountability for business results as well as effectiveness.

At the Interpersonal Level

If we are not accountable to each other in our work relationships, they may remain broken for some time and adversely affect the team's overall functioning, its credibility, and/or its integrity. The team needs a process to fix broken relationships that affect its success.

At the Individual Level

The consequences to us for not holding ourselves accountable can be substantial. If we are "out of integrity," sooner or later it will catch up with us in our work relationships. In a Collaborative Workplace, the accountable individual seeks coaching, counseling, or other supportive services to grow through the behaviors and attitudes that are creating the disconnects.

Agreement 15: Amendments/Renewal

Nothing is ever cast in concrete except our principles and values. Because we need the flexibility to risk, learn, and grow, we can amend our Operating Agreements at any time, as long as consensus is used in arriving at the amendments. Oftentimes, team members will go through this process over the period of several weeks or months, begin behaving accordingly, and try to adapt the agreements to real work circumstances. Then they find out they either do not fully understand how to implement them, did not fully understand what they had agreed to, or now disagree and want to revise them. There needs to be an open agenda item allowing every member the right to bring up an amendment at any time.

With time, even the best teams begin to take their agreements for granted. After about four to six months, the group gradually begins to forget what they agreed to. Situations emerge that challenge the group's memory as to what they have agreed to, and often they slip. Keep the agreements in front of the team at every meeting. Within 24 months, the agreements may lose some of their relevance. There will be new people on the team with new dynamics and needs. There will be new issues and work relationships. Products and services will have changed. Customer needs will have changed. It will be time to review and renew. Use a blank sheet process to renew the Operating Agreements every two years.

The Operating Agreements Process

Imagine a team sitting in a room for two to four days of facilitated work creating its Operating Agreements. Both inside the room and out, members of the team engage in substantive conversations about meanings of terms, values, beliefs, and how they want to be treated by each other. The conversation gets heated at times, funny sometimes, and serious at other times. At one point there is a significant difference of view on a topic and a member digs in his heels. People complain that it is taking forever to get the agreements completed. Breaks, meals, and off-line conversations do not seem to dissuade the dissenting member from his position; the team feels it has reached an impasse. After two hours, many are ready to strangle the dissenter, but know that it might have been them (and could be in future). So they make a conscious decision to persist.

Carefully and skillfully the team narrows the gap in the differences and works through each of what some feel are petty or technical issues. Still it is not enough. The process goes on for another hour. It is not working. The tension rises again. Some personal things are said about the dissenting member. There is a strong reaction. Then, out of desperation, the team uses some tools in its collaborative tool kit that allow it to get behind all the objections to the dissenter's core issues. They are emotional. They represent experiences and pain this person had five years ago when he first joined the company. Having really been heard and respected, with the root cause discovered, the member's resistance dissipates and the agreement is reached in a matter of minutes.

What was needed for the team to be successful? Patience. Persistence. Empathic listening. A total commitment to the success of the process. Tolerance for one another's differences and styles. Some tools. And a skilled, resourceful facilitator. It worked.

The results were on several levels:

- *Culture.* The team agreed to a set of values that represented what was important and unique to it as a group and how it would operate. It now owns them and will be responsible for their implementation. Through this experience of struggle and discovery, a new level of trust has been created, and integrity and respect for each other have been demonstrably increased; a collaborative culture has been created.
- *Process.* The team members know they can work through their differences with one another; confidence has risen.
- *Content.* The team has its Operating Agreements. This situa-

tion points to some critical success factors that enable the process to work.

Critical Success Factors

There is a pattern among teams that have successfully created and implemented their Operating Agreements. Five critical success factors have been identified.

Key Rules

First, all agreements must be reached with true consensus. Second, everyone who is on the team and has to live by the agreements must be there in person. The process cannot be done over the phone or by proxy. No substitutions. Third, a skilled facilitator is needed to work the team through the process. It is essential to honor these three key rules.

Giving It All the Time It Needs

As one member said at a leadership team meeting, "The thing about Operating Agreements is that you either pay now or pay later, but you will pay. The choice you have is not whether you will pay, but what you want to pay and when." You pay up-front in terms of time, or you pay later in terms of lost productivity, tension, anger, conflict, and loss of team spirit.

In our culture there is a lot of pressure to "just do it"—fast. In this context, Operating Agreements are at best seen as just another content task which, if tackled quickly, can be done in less than an hour, and at worst might be an obstacle to the team's success. This approach will not result in a collaborative culture nor significantly improve the team's efficiency or effectiveness.

We are shifting the culture from one of independent action, competition, and conflict to one of mutual accountability, collaboration, and learning. It takes time for people to realign their expectations of themselves and each other. Normally it takes two to four days to get the initial set of agreements developed, but several months to ensure that behaviors are consistent with the agreements. If the team takes shortcuts, the process will not work. It is deliberate and structured and "takes whatever time it takes" for the team members to work through their differences with each other.

Struggle and Discovery

The process of creating a team's Operating Agreements is perhaps the most important start-up activity the team members can engage in. It is in their struggle with one another and in their discovery of how they can work through their differences that they learn a whole new level of honesty, candor, and trust. Trust is the glue that holds any organization together.

By actively engaging in the struggle with our own assumptions about how to manage a business, challenging those assumptions, and then redefining them so we all win, we can break through the shackles of the hierarchical paradigm and establish a whole new level of relationship, trust, and work effectiveness.

Tolerance for Ambiguity and Adversity

As we saw in the team example above, it is critical that when one or more members of a team are having difficulty about a particular decision, agreement, or issue, the others rally around them, listen, and create a shared understanding of the issue and its resolution. In confronting our own intolerance for others, we learn about ourselves. In our impatience with the ambiguity of creating a new culture, we come face-to-face with what drives and motivates each of us. As with a "hung jury," it is when we are ready to walk out on the team that we absolutely have to keep our feet in the room and work through our differences. That is how we discover ourselves, our strength as a team, and the power of true collaboration.

Integrity and Completeness

You might hear people say, "Let's do it in one day. Let's do a 'straw thought' off-line, bring it in, process it, and get our agreements completed more quickly. I trust you guys to get it right. After all, we've known each other a long time and have always worked well with each other." These statements are more often the rule than the exception, and provide a challenge to the team sponsor of the process and the facilitator.

For example, one team that took a shortcut by having two members create a straw thought actually ended spending more time. When it was presented, team members began to take strong exception to the thinking and assumptions of the two individuals. In another team, the members had known each other for 15 years, but when they got into the process, they quickly realized that they did not know each other as well as they thought.

No Shortcuts

Operating Agreements have to be experienced to be owned and to have value. We are not creating pop art culture. It is not a superficial process. We are engaged in the creation of the new cultural foundation for building trust, mutual respect, and individual value. Trust takes time. We get the behavior we create, so we must create it carefully.

Recommendations for Creating Operating Agreements

Whether the team is cross-functional or single-function, project-based or long-term, new or old, ad hoc or permanent, the following recommendations apply as the team begins its work:

• *Ensuring clear sponsor direction.* Be sure you have clear direction and a charter from your team sponsor. This charter should define the task, the deliverables, and any boundary conditions, such as time, money, and use of other resources. Periodic meetings with the sponsor ensure alignment and avoid disconnects down the line.

• *Preparing for the process.* Identify a skilled facilitator who understands group and team dynamics and the collaborative process. Find a location on-site or off-site where the team will be undisturbed during the process. This will take two to four days, and may occur in several sessions over a period of time, so it is best if the same location can be used. It must be quiet and keep members free from any distractions.

- *Conducting the process.* Apply the critical success factors previously noted as you move through the agreements process. Flipchart everything and create a working "memory" of the results to ensure that you are all agreeing to the same thing. Clarify meanings of words to avoid misunderstandings.

- *After the process.* Once the initial agreements are completed, post them on the wall in front of the team at each meeting. Some teams put them on a laminated card. After three months, review the agreements to see how they are working. A meeting should be dedicated to evaluating your experience, making upgrades, and recommitting to the agreements.

Summary

Trust is the glue in the new work environment. But how do we get it, and if we have it, how do we keep it? Trust is an outcome in our relationships; it is something that results in the workplace when everyone's behavior is based on the core values of the Collaborative Work Ethic. There are three fundamental ingredients that must be present if there is to be trust in the workplace. First, there needs to be a recognition that the *culture* must change. Authority and command no longer work in producing high-performance organizations. Second, there needs to be a willingness on the part of management to create a new *covenant* with the workforce, a covenant based on the core values of collaboration. Third, the members of teams and groups of all kinds across the organization need to engage in the creation of their new culture by establishing Operating Agreements based on true *consensus*. In this way, we move beyond the games and techniques used to acquire and use power, beyond dysfunction and conflict in our relationships, and toward a workplace of trust, integrity, and authentic, genuine relationships. In this new environment, our new workplace culture becomes an asset and not a liability. We finally get to collaborate internally and compete externally.

4

Collaborative Leadership

The first responsibility of a leader is to define reality. The last is to say thank you. In between the two, the leader must become a servant and a debtor.

—*Max DePree,* Leadership Is an Art

It was time for the consulting assignment with the information systems leadership team to end. The consultants had done what they had set out to do: The organization's culture, work processes, and structure had been transformed into a collaborative, team-based business focusing on the customer. In the close-out meeting, one of the questions was: Who is the leader? Who will carry forward the momentum? Who will identify the interventions needed, be the catalyst, and ensure there is follow-through?

The answer was not expected: "We are the leader!" "How can that be?" they were asked. The response was insightful. Henry said, "If Jeff isn't here, we miss his ability to challenge whether we are headed in the right direction. If Sarah isn't here, we miss her facilitation skills and interventions. If John isn't here, we miss his analytic thinking and way of keeping our feet on the ground. In fact," Henry added with a laugh, "if John isn't here, we know his thinking well enough to anticipate the kinds of questions he'd raise, ask them, and then check back with him when he returns." As Henry continued, acknowledging what each individual brought to the team, the message was clear: *Leadership is a function performed by many, not a position held by one.* It is no longer acceptable to demand or mandate. We must include, engage, and inspire.

In the Collaborative Workplace, anyone can be a leader at any given point. Leadership as a function is situational; it depends on circumstances and not on position, power, or authority. This notion of leadership presents us with a paradox. In our current mind-set, leaders are expected to tell us what to do. They rise through the ranks as a result of their expertise, skills, and ability to manage corporate politics. In the collaborative mind-set, people in leadership roles are expected to engage the workforce in building ownership for the company's strategic direction, to be part of a flatter structure, and to build open and trust-based work relationships. As a leader, what are my new roles? How am I supposed to behave? If I am willing to change, how do I shift from the hierarchical mind-set to the collaborative approach?

This chapter is designed to explore these questions. We will first look at the mind-set shift needed to function effectively in the new work environment. Then we will consider the roles and responsibilities of collaborative leaders and follow it with a discussion of the behaviors that are expected of the new leadership. Finally, we will suggest a series of steps you can take to discover whether the collaborative path is for you.

Shifting the Leadership Mind-Set

Old habits die hard. Hierarchical thinking is a deeply embedded mind-set. For many of us, it represents how we have come to view ourselves and a lifetime of habits on how we get ahead in the world. It is difficult to change behaviors, attitudes, and leadership styles. In fact, the pain of not changing usually needs to be greater than the pain of changing if there is to be any shift at all. It is a very personal decision, but one that can be thoughtfully considered. Let's look at some key elements of this mind-set shift.

Recognizing Many Leaders, Not Just One

Our culture is geared toward the identification and development of "heroic" leaders, men and women who will provide us direction and rescue us in difficult times. Even when children are as young as two or three years old, you can hear preschool teachers say,

"That child is a leader." We place an extraordinarily high value on leadership based in authority, either informal or personal. But in valuing the role of the leader, we sometimes confirm our own dependency and validate the view that we ourselves are not responsible for outcomes. We can fall into the trap of seeing leadership as a position held by one person rather than a function shared by many people whose leadership abilities will emerge as needed. Unfortunately, by buying into what can be called the "Assumption of One Leader," we can tacitly disempower ourselves and one another.

We have also built into our work culture an even more disempowering assertion: "Lead, follow, or get out of the way." This homily portrays a work culture that is effectively victimizing itself by the assumption of one leader, that says:

- There are leaders and there are followers, and they are never the same people.
- In every organization or group there is one leader; we have chosen that leader for his or her expertise, wisdom, or skill; we must give that leader a chance to succeed or fail.
- Leadership equals authority equals control equals power.
- Only one person should and can be held accountable.
- Leaders get paid to make the tough decisions.
- We must defer to the leader even if that person is headed in the wrong direction; it is not my responsibility.
- It is unwise to challenge leadership unless you are ready to look for another job.

The net effect of the Assumption of One is not only to disempower the workforce but to put a cap on the productive capacity of the company. This Assumption tells the workforce that they are not in charge and have little value. It disregards the inherent leadership capacities of other team members and delivers the message that each individual has only certain skills and should stick to a particular role.

The reality of leadership, particularly in the global marketplace, is that it is a function, not a position. It is a "we," requiring the full application of many people's skills and talents, both as leaders and as followers, to ensure the success of the organization. Everyone has a piece of the leadership pie, and everyone is valued.

In the Collaborative Workplace, leadership is being redefined using a different assumption, the Assumption of Many. In this assumption, each of us has leadership qualities that emerge when the right moment arises for us. Leadership is situational and evolves over time as we learn to take on more and more responsibility.

Giving Up Control and Engaging the Heart and Spirit

The vice president for information systems at the DyNex Corporation looked out over her spectacles and said: "I have worked very hard for 20 years to get where I am. I've sacrificed everything. Now we're making a profit, and I'll be damned if I am going to give up control now." It was true. She had been through a lot to get her title, responsibilities, and respect. She had 500 people reporting to her, and because work was her life, it really did feel to her as though collaborative leadership meant giving up control.

CEO Dennis Longstreet of Ortho Biotech feels that when you start a change process, you give up the ability to make firm, hard decisions and take a chance that employees may lead you where you don't want to go. But most of the workforce want the same things managers want because "everyone wants to succeed." Giving up control is what it feels like. We assume we must have a tight rein on things or the company will not be efficient. If we give up control, this logic says, we are more likely to fail, and that is not acceptable. Besides, other people cannot be trusted to do the job right, even though they are bright. Bonuses and the future depend on doing the job right.

In a work culture based on the Assumption of One, a leader expects total control and the prerogatives that go along with it. Control is something always retained. It is the leader's choice whether or not to give it away or delegate it. As one corporate team said as it was trying to decide how it would make strategic decisions, "If all else fails, we will give the decision back to our manager."

But does top management really have control, or is it just an illusion? Think back to our basic assumptions in Chapter 2 about how work gets done. It is the workforce that decides how the work gets done, no matter what leader thinks he or she is in control. The Collaborative Workplace recognizes that, in reality, control rests with everyone in the organization. Leaders have influence; very few have the degree of control they think they have. As a result, the ability to effectively direct the organization is a function of the leader's ability to engage the workforce, to build value, and to coach, support, and guide people to achieve the desired results. This process requires new understandings, skills, and capabilities. Control, in the Collaborative Workplace, is a shared responsibility.

Offloading the Structure-First Mind-Set

The executive of a Fortune 500 corporation used the strategic planning retreat to survey the company's market position. One clear conclusion was that the organization was losing market leadership to companies that were far more efficient and better strategized. The company's profits were declining, its market share was off 5 percent, and its key customers were talking about leaving. What should it do?

Using what I will call a *structure-first mind-set*, the executive would see the problem as reducing costs in the short term to achieve long-term competitive advantage. Accordingly, the CEO would order layoffs as well as a reorganization of the business' core functions. The company would probably call in a big management consulting house, ask for a study, and implement many or all of its recommendations. Throughout, the objective would be short-term cost reduction and sending out a clear signal that this executive was about action and results. Nine times out of ten, achieving those results would entail some form of structural change: reorganizing, flattening the organization, reengineering, downsizing, or outsourcing.

Many members of the workforce would call this type of structural change "the program of the month" or "rearranging the deck chairs on the Titanic." To the executive with a structure-first mind-set, however, reducing the headcount would be perfectly justified by the market. The CEO would feel that this was no time for "soft" approaches that took forever. This was the time for action—"just do it." The executive would probably endorse ample communication, a severance package, outplacement, and other support services, but the goal and net effect would be straightforward: a significant reduction in the workforce.

Another look at this approach might produce a different interpretation, and this executive might be seen as highly reactive, even as flailing in the wind. Often the structure-first approach sets in motion a downward spiral of reduced productivity, lowered confidence, lost credibility, and diminished customer service, which ultimately result in even more reductions as customers take their business elsewhere. Sometimes these actions do not even produce short-term profit.

One communications company terminated thousands of people just last year, and there was no impact on the bottom line; other parts of the business soaked up the savings. The company is now in its fifth wave of staff reductions in as many years, cutting several thousand more this year as the board becomes increasingly restive.

Another manufacturing company has been doing what we might call "structuring down" for 10 years, to the point where 75 percent of its original workforce is gone. Productivity among the survivors has dropped, and the business base is quickly evaporating. Management fell into the trap that its problems could be solved by structural change. The company may even be forced into chapter 11 bankruptcy.

The challenge, then, for the emerging collaborative leader is to move beyond the structure-first assumptions about how best to lead and manage a business. There *is* an alternative—what I call the *culture-first mind-set*—in which our decisions are driven by principles and core values rather than by power or personality. This mind-set is based on the following key assumptions:

- The only real short-term solution is to plan for the long term; short-term gain often becomes long-term pain.
- The most effective way to reduce cost is to increase the productivity of the company's workforce.
- To increase productivity, the workforce must be engaged in solving the problems of the business.
- If there must be a reduction in force, the people affected should be actively engaged in the process.

Figure 4–1. Comparison of structure-first and culture-first mind-sets.

Structure-First	Culture-First
• Focus is on the short term	• Focus is on the long term
• Focus is on the debit side of the ledger	• Focus is on the asset side of the ledger
• Approach is top-down, imposed	• Approach is engaged, collaborative
• Treats workforce as not responsible	• Assumes workforce is fully responsible
• Focus is on strategic/tactical and operational levels	• Focus is on collaborative and transformative processes

Figure 4–1 provides a comparison of structure-first and culture-first mind-sets.

Behavioral Transformation

We are not talking about behavior modification. We are talking about behavioral *transformation*. Does this require a personality transplant? Not at all. What it does require is a recognition that in a Collaborative Workplace the old ways of behaving and relating no longer apply. Perhaps the most difficult thing for anyone—especially a senior executive who has made it to the top using the old paradigm—is to transform his or her leadership style. What a leader can do is commit to a personal growth process that will map out the path toward a more collaborative leadership style. One such process, the *personal journey,* will be described later in this chapter.

Before making this journey, however, we must be very clear about its difficulties. Figure 4–2 suggests that the beliefs manifested in our leading and managing philosophies are deeply rooted and not easily changed. Our beliefs have been in the mak-

Figure 4–2. Shifting a mind-set.

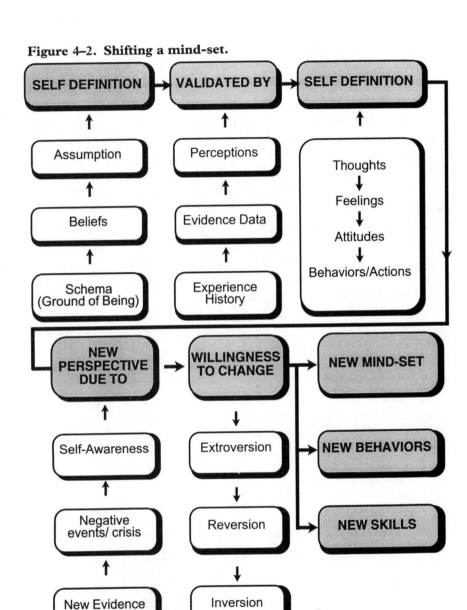

ing since childhood, formed by our successes, experiences, history, difficult lessons, and pain—i.e., our very ground of being. These events and experiences shape and drive our behavior throughout our lives. Our educational processes and initial work experiences reinforce the mind-set by stressing the importance of control, authority, discipline, competition, and decisiveness. There is little emphasis on the importance of effective relationships, joint problem solving, and collaboration. Add to this basic outlook a reward system that incents us to produce financial results above all else, and one can see how fundamentally difficult a mind-set shift can be.

Life-changing experiences like a heart attack, a divorce, or being fired from a job usually have a profound impact on us and can play a critical role in how we behave in the future, particularly when under pressure or when we find ourselves in a similar situation. But the pain of not changing must be greater than the pain of changing. There must be good reason, or good arguments, for someone to alter his or her way of doing things. The realities of the new business world are that reason. They point clearly to the need for a fundamental realignment in leadership style if we are to remain competitive. Change is possible if the individual is willing to face the new realities, observe his or her own behavior, and make commitments to realign and behave differently. There is less value placed on lofty statements and good intentions. In the Collaborative Workplace, what matters is the willingness to change, adopt new behaviors, and maintain effective relationships.

The Roles and Responsibilities of the Collaborative Leader

Mary was confused about her new job. "Usually," she said, "as team leader, I delegate the jobs to the team members and I supervise their completion, setting standards and providing moral support and motivation. I don't understand what this new job is. Where is my authority? Who reports to me? Who am I accountable to?"

It used to be so simple. Everyone knew what the rules were, and climbing the ladder to leadership was the result of knowledge, expertise, and politics. Now the rules have changed, and there is much discomfort. In fact, most leaders today who are trying something new will tell you that the new approaches to management take them way outside their comfort zones. At Goretex, they have even gone so far as to call their approach "unmanagement."

In the Collaborative Workplace, the organization is led and managed by people working in teams, building on the symbol of the circle rather than the pyramid. In this organizational design, there are four basic kinds of Collaborative Teams that need the leadership function:

- *Strategic leadership team (SLT).* Provides overall strategic direction and guidance to a company, department, or unit.
- *Functional team.* A standing group that has a designated functional responsibility and is tied into the SLT. Functional teams may also have subgroups called *natural work groups.* These are groups of people clustered by geography or task in manageable units.
- *Project team.* A temporary grouping of people who are working together on a specific task. It may last from a few days to a year or more. Often, members have more than one team responsibility.
- *Cross-functional team (CFT).* A temporary or permanent team of people who come together across the boundaries of specific departments to focus on a customer need or concern common to the entire organization.

In the Collaborative Workplace, there is no team boss. However, in most of these collaborative teams, there is usually a designated contact person who can speak for the team.

Whether the organization is totally collaborative, totally hierarchical, or evolving from hierarchy to collaboration, the collaborative leader must be aware of a wide range of functions to be performed, many of which need to be fulfilled simultaneously. Here are the core functions:

- *The leader as sponsor.* The sponsor of any team, particularly a leadership team, provides air cover and strategic direction for the team; provides the resources, initial charter, and boundary conditions for the activity; provides coaching support for functional team leaders and monitors the process to ensure its success; helps maintain the integrity of the team's operating processes; and makes necessary interventions.

- *The leader as facilitator.* The facilitator ensures that meetings, team dynamics, and interpersonal relationships function effectively; provides meeting design and implementation services; manages preventions and interventions; ensures internal coordination of activities among team members; protects the integrity of the team process; and works with the sponsor if there are problems.

- *The leader as coach.* This function requires objectivity about individuals and their roles in the team/organization. It is a supportive role, one that involves providing guidance and being a sounding board.

- *The leader as change agent/catalyst.* This function requires a very great level of objectivity about the organization, teams, and team members. It requires the ability to hold individuals accountable for their actions, to make unpopular observations, and to energize a group to action, enabling breakthroughs where possible.

- *The leader as healer.* Most organizations have a lot of pain stored up in them about broken relationships and broken processes. In this role, the leader plays the role of mediator and catalyst in bringing people together, ensuring integrity in work relationships, and making necessary interventions.

- *The leader as member.* At one or more points, even "natural leaders" will simply serve as members of the team, taking full responsibility for the success of the team; actively participating in its activities; nurturing and supporting the team's development; doing the work; and living up to the team's governance processes.

- *The leader as manager/administrator.* This traditional role involves the daily administrative responsibilities, processes, and systems essential to managing the boundaries with the larger organization or key stakeholders. It may also involve administrative action affecting individuals if coaching and mediation do not work.

Critical to the success of the leadership function in any Collaborative Workplace is that all these roles are fulfilled.

Collaborative Behaviors

The senior executive at CYLOR, a large distribution company, thought he was doing all the right things by flattening his organization, reengineering key business processes, and delegating full responsibility to 20 senior people he called "cluster leaders." They were empowered, he said, to fully implement the vision, mission, and strategic direction of the company, unfettered by central controls. They must not supervise; rather, they must be coaches and mentors for their subordinates, who were not really their subordinates, but their colleagues. (But they were not really colleagues, either, because they reported both to the cluster leaders and to the senior executive.)

Sound confusing? It certainly was to the cluster leaders. The CEO's intentions were moving in the right direction. What was missing were clear expectations, clear roles and responsibilities, and sufficient organization, management, and skills support to ensure their success. Most importantly, accountability was not clear. In the headlong rush to become self-managed and empowered, CYLOR's executive was making a very critical mistake—failing to distinguish between the leadership role and the leadership function. Each leader was essentially thrown into the ocean of empowerment without a life raft. The result was that many were in danger of drowning. There was a backlash. Within six months, the cluster leaders became de facto regional vice presidents, each operating in a different way, creating redundancy, and increasing costs. There was a loss of credibility, and the opportunity to start the process of empowering people within some kind of structured process suffered irreparable damage.

Central to the success of any significant growth or change effort designed to increase flexibility and competitiveness is the establishment of clear expectations about behavior. In the Collaborative Workplace, collaborative leaders are expected to behave differently in thought, feeling, and spirit. I like to think of these three areas as behaviors from the head, the heart, and the spirit.

Behaviors From the Head

Behaviors from the head are based on rational analysis, bottom-line numbers, systems thinking, and efficiency. In the hierarchy paradigm, this means a focus on control, accountability, cost, and the short term. There is a focus on the debit, or cost, side of the corporate ledger, rather than on the asset, human capital, or productivity side of the ledger. In the Collaborative Workplace, the expectations are different. Collaborative leaders are expected to do the following:

- To ensure *strategic alignment* among all the key stakeholders in the organization, with customers, and with the market
- To ensure *congruence* among all elements of the organization, with a focus on its internal processes and integrity
- To create and support a learning environment that encourages *risk taking* and enables people to make some mistakes without fear of reprisal
- To create and sustain organizational *momentum* in the company's growth and development
- To focus the energy of the workforce on *results,* both in terms of the firm's economics and in terms of the quality of its product, work relationships, and customer satisfaction
- To use *measurement* to monitor the company's progress toward strategic objectives in all areas of the business
- To proactively and regularly sponsor *renewal* of the Operating Agreements and work processes that ensure the highest level of effectiveness in relationships, results, and reputation

Behaviors From the Heart

Behaviors from the heart emanate from the psychological and social side of leaders and focus on relationships, respect for others, and the elements of motivation. In a hierarchy, the attention depends on the individual and is found in the human resources function, which has responsibility for training, wellness, and social support programs. In the Collaborative Workplace, these responsibilities belong to line leaders, managers, and teams. Behaviors from the heart are front and center. Collaborative leaders are expected to do as follows:

- To show their *value for people* by walking the talk, building those behaviors around a basic respect for the dignity and esteem of every individual
- To provide inspiration for the workforce to achieve *a sense of common purpose* by continuing to build value for and ownership of a shared vision, mission, and strategic direction
- To create a *nurturing work environment* in which members take care of each other and the team
- To encourage an environment in which people can expect *forgiveness* for their mistakes while also holding each other responsible and accountable for them
- To support a commitment by everyone in the organization to build and sustain *whole relationships,* in which issues are resolved quickly and completely
- To create a sense of community and *mutual support*
- To provide *acknowledgment* through a system of rewards and recognition that supports individual and team accomplishments, their effectiveness, and the quality of their work
- To ensure *recommitment* by each member and team to perform at the company's highest level

Behaviors From the Spirit

Behaviors from the spirit derive from the spiritual and philosophic side of collaborative leaders and speak to their core values, beliefs, motivations, and perspectives on how organizations and people work. In a homogeneous culture, these values and beliefs tend to be generally accepted. In the Collaborative Workplace, in which the culture is far more diverse in terms of style, ethnicity, and values, collaborative leaders create a common ground, based on principle, that will speak to the basic needs of everyone in the workforce. Collaborative leaders are expected:

- To honor and enhance the *self-esteem and dignity of each individual*, regardless of characteristics or origin. Similarly, *team-*

esteem will also be honored and respected as a core building block for ensuring long-term effectiveness.

- To wholly commit to *integrity,* both in their own behavior and in the organization's work, practice, processes, growth, and development.
- To build an *environment of trust,* in which people can earn or regain the confidence and trust of their colleagues.

Becoming a Collaborative Leader

The true test of leadership is the ability to see your own self-imposed limitations and to break through to a new sense of yourself that transforms your attitudes, behaviors, and approach to working with others.

Most people who seriously consider making a fundamental shift in their approach to leadership rarely do so because they woke up one morning and said, "Today I think I will transform myself." Usually there is some significant event, or series of events in their personal life or that of their company, that punctuates the necessity for a dramatic change in style. Some people take this personal journey out of a desire to try a new approach to leading and managing. Others see the trends, recognize the new realities for what they are, and—either out of altruism, good sense, or an instinct for survival—actively seek out the new methodologies.

But whatever motivates the journey, it is an ongoing commitment you make to yourself to confront your best and worst parts to produce a breakthrough result that transforms your attitudes, behaviors, and approach to working with others. It is not a one-time event. In a Collaborative Workplace, it is a journey toward true collaborative leadership.

Preparing for the Journey: A Ten-Step Process

Before you set off, there must be a clear commitment to complete the journey. This commitment is critical because, in the course of the trip, you will be getting feedback you may not want to hear, feedback that may challenge the assumptions you have had about yourself and present an alternative picture of who you think you are. The journey requires a conscious decision that you are willing to explore your capacity to lead others into the next century collaboratively. Here are some tips to help get you started:

- Create a loose-leaf journal to record the steps you take and the observations you and others make.
- Get a coach—a friend, colleague, spouse, or even a counselor—who will support you through the journey. It is important to have an objective set of eyes looking at the data you will generate.
- Create a road map and put it on a timeline. This process needs some time definition to it.
- Write it all down; this makes it real.

Step 1: Analyzing Your Core Values

The first step is to find out what makes you tick. Write down what you value and why. What are your beliefs, and where did they come from? Are they still valid? What is your motivation? What really drives you? This analysis should produce a very clear picture of your values profile, and provide the foundation for your approach to leadership. Now compare your values profile with the new realities in your environment. Given your values, what leadership behaviors do you use? How do others see your behaviors? What is working and what is not?

Step 2: Assessing Your Skills

Identify your greatest strengths and areas for growth. In a section of your journal, create a sheet for each of the following areas of your life: education, work, family, religious commitment, social interaction, community and/or political involvement, financial picture, athletic skills, and cultural interests. On each sheet, in five-year increments, write down your specific accomplishments—things you actually did. Allow yourself some time to complete this step. It is often difficult to remember everything you've accomplished. Ask family and friends to help you with this. Once you have completed this diagnostic, look for patterns across the years and translate them into specific skills and competencies you have: e.g., project-oriented; analytic; committed to community service.

Pull out the skills and capabilities you have that relate to the workplace. Compare them to the requirements of a collaborative leader and determine where you want to invest time developing new skills (developing facilitation and coaching skills, for example).

Step 3: Formulating Your Vision and Mission

You are now ready to formulate your own personal vision and mission statements that will govern who you are and what you do for the next several years of your life. It is often said "to thine own self be true," and in this search for your true, current identity, you will discover whether there is congruence between your values and what you are trying to accomplish in your life. You have to really ask yourself whether all the things you have been putting up with to get to this position in life are really worth it. You may find out, and many do, that they simply are not. Critical decisions about the future of your job are often made at this point to sustain your personal integrity.

Step 4: Redefining Your Leading and Managing Philosophy

The result of this step is the redefinition of your approach to working with others. Given that a major part of this journey is transcending the old paradigm, this can be difficult. The rubber begins to hit the road. It is no longer theoretical. Now it's personal. An important tool here is wide-ranging feedback from your peers, teammates, subordinates, and superiors, to give you a comprehensive perspective on how you actually behave. Using this feedback, you can pinpoint any incongruence between the principles of collaborative leadership and how you've actually been doing up to this point.

Step 5: Assessing Your Behavior

Using these data, begin to identify the specific results of your behavior in the workplace. Does it square with how you want to be viewed by yourself and others? What is the cost to you, to them, and to the company? The purpose of this step is to provide you with a choice in how you want to behave in the future, and to help you begin mapping a course of action that will enable you to align your values with your actions.

Step 6: Analyzing Your Roles

Refer back to the seven leadership roles and responsibilities identified earlier in this chapter. Given your profile, which of these roles will you now play? What skills do you need in order to be successful at them?

Step 7: Making the Choice

With the analysis complete, you can choose how you will behave, acquire the skills you need, and measure your progress. The act of choosing is itself an essential step in abandoning the old paradigm. In our experience, choosing is not a one-time action. Hundreds of choices need to be made each week to produce a lasting major change.

Step 8: Setting Measurements and Recommitting Yourself

Set some measures and benchmarks for yourself. Ask your coach to give you feedback on a regular basis. Recognize that you will make mistakes. Give yourself a break by learning from them and recommitting to your new approach to leadership. Most importantly, believe in yourself.

Step 9: Implementing Your Action Plan

Now is the time to convert analysis, self-discovery, and choices into an action plan and then implement it. This is another place at which many travelers get stopped. It means experimenting and trying new ways of behaving. It is scary sometimes. People you have worked with for years may not trust it. The trick is to persevere.

Step 10: Evaluating and Celebrating Your Progress

After three months, take stock of your progress. Use your measures to evaluate your wins and losses. Create your road map for the next three months and, whatever you do, celebrate your experience with your coach, teammates, spouse, and friends.

Summary

The new realities in business require a new type of leadership. Command-and-control no longer applies. Collaborative leadership, however, requires a significant shift in our relationships in the workplace. Since leadership is no longer a position but a function, and since everyone can be a leader, the responsibility for leading the organization shifts to the entire workforce. The traditional roles and responsibilities of leadership also change—from commanding to coaching, from telling to engaging, and from delegating to others to working with others. Our behaviors must change as we learn how to function in an environment of consensus formation, conflict resolution, and full responsibility. This is not an easy transformation. In fact, to shift the mind-set from hierarchical to collaborative leadership requires each of us to discover our own capacities and skills and to map out a personal plan of action that will enable us to achieve our goals.

5

Building Strategic Business Alignment

Even if you think you are on the right track, you'll get run over if you just sit there.

—Will Rogers

It was clear to the president that Stahlcote, Inc., needed to redirect its market focus. He knew the competition had recently found a new way to manufacture its product and as a result had captured 12 percent of Stahlcote's market in just the last 24 months. The trend was clear. Immediate action was essential.

The executive team was brought together for a three-day strategic planning retreat. The urgency of the meeting was evident as everyone scrambled to pull the data together. The mood was similar to the one that had prevailed during the merger two years ago, when the need to take immediate action had seemed to overwhelm logic. The retreat focused on re-visioning the company's strategic direction and the immediate actions that had to be taken. When it ended, everyone had his or her assignment and a 90-day time line to produce results. The president ended the retreat by saying: "My friends, our future depends on you. Let's just *do* it!"

The team members went back to their respective organizations and announced the changes. Some laid people off. Others cut budgets, and an aggressive marketing campaign was kicked off. While the structural changes were being implemented the grumble rate skyrocketed and productivity plummeted as the employees began to feel the impact. Three months later, sales had still not increased, although cost reductions had been achieved. Productivity remained low. Anxiety was up. It was difficult to get midlevel managers to speak at meetings or be enthusiastic about their assignments. The malaise continued for another year until the board finally hired a new president. His first official act was to hold a strategic planning retreat.

Breaking the Crisis Cycle
Through Collaboration

This story is being played out all across the country as one company after another tries to avoid getting run over, searches for an enhanced market niche, or seeks to refocus the productive energies of its people. In the process, many companies create their own crisis cycle. It begins when a company needs immediate results and does not have time to plan long term. As people focus on the short term, they produce results that have little to do with the long-term success of the company, thus repeating the crisis cycle. Without an effective method to produce strategic focus, crisis actually becomes the modus operandi, with leadership frequently mobilizing its workforce to take swift tactical action in hopes that it will produce a different strategic result. Such short-term actions are often implemented without building sufficient buy-in, resulting in poor results that lead in turn to another round of cost cutting.

Whether the company is in crisis mode or simply needs to redirect its market focus, the worst thing it can do is demand a short-term turnaround to a problem that has evolved over years— particularly if it imposes the changes from above, without significant involvement of the workforce responsible for implementing them. This approach can result in shifting the business focus to mere survival and finger-pointing.

There *is* a collaborative method that can break the crisis cycle by mobilizing the workforce, building value for a new direction, and refocusing the company's energy. Called the Strategic Alignment Method, it is a principle-based process that ensures alignment among the company's key stakeholders for the new focus. Just as Operating Agreements are a vehicle for redefining the culture and behaviors of the Collaborative Workplace, the Strategic

Alignment Method gives the organization its business identity, ensures that it is customer-focused, clarifies its unique and value-added role in the market, and provides a rational framework for tactical actions that reflect the true strategic position of the company in the marketplace.

This chapter describes the elements of the Strategic Alignment Method and shows the specific steps needed to move a business from reactive approaches and short-term planning to proactive, long-term strategic growth. It first describes the method, defining the terms and the benefits. It then outlines the phases and steps of the method, using as an example the experiences of Stahlcote's employees as they work to reenergize their organization.

The Strategic Alignment Method

Like a rocket, every organization needs a guidance system, a booster with plenty of fuel, and a mission-control center to ensure the success of the entire enterprise. In Chapter 3 we talked about the rocket booster—the organization's culture. In Chapter 6 (and again in Chapter 9) we will talk about the control center, the systems and supports required to make the launch successful. Our focus now is on the guidance system that ensures that the business hits its market target with the greatest accuracy possible.

Every organization needs to be strategically aligned if it is to succeed in the market. To get the full power of the rocket booster, however, it must be focused on pursuing its unique and value-added role in the market and on building value among all of its stakeholders for moving in this direction. To this end it needs to harness the power of collaboration to the difficult tasks of identifying the company's market niche and meeting customer requirements. For this purpose, the executives at Stahlcote created a cross-functional strategic alignment team.

What Strategic Alignment Means

Alignment is defined as follows: "to be in or come into precise adjustment or correct relative position." *Strategic* is defined as "of great importance within an integrated whole or to a planned effect." In the Collaborative Workplace, *strategic alignment* is the process that enables the entire organization to come to a basic agreement on a definition of its unique and value-added role in the marketplace; to identify customer requirements; and to determine the company's competitive advantage and strategies for growth. This means that all the key stakeholders agree to what the organization has decided to do. The stakeholders include the customers, the shareholders, the board of directors, the executive leadership, the membership of the organization, the suppliers/vendors, and the community they operate in. The specific stakeholders and their relative importance to the direction of the organization will vary.

The Benefits of the Strategic Alignment Method

There are four critical benefits that come from using this method annually (or whenever a major market challenge faces the organization).

1. *Building full-value customer relationships.* When a Collaborative Workplace is strategically aligned, it is totally focused on customers and their requirements. We know their business, their specific needs for our products/services, and the advantages we bring to them. We then build a collaborative, ongoing relationship with them, leading to what we can call a *full-value* contract.

A full-value contract is a document between the company and its customers that spells out how they are going to work together to achieve the full value of their relationship. It is their charter and their set of Operating Agreements. The full-value contract gives customers an opportunity to specifically address their needs and concerns in a way that ensures that the supplier will listen. It provides a platform for ongoing dialogue and responsiveness. Measures are put in place to assess responsiveness and the effectiveness of the relationship. The full-value contract also benefits the supplier of the product or service because it focuses the supplier on the customer and provides an ongoing planning process, increasing understanding of the product/service being provided, improving communications, and facilitating problem solving and conflict resolution.

2. *Assessing the company's unique and value-added role.* When a company is entering a new market, developing a new product, reacting to new competition, or refocusing its strategic direction, no area is more important than its strategic focus and direction. Many companies believe that they know who they are and how they are viewed by the marketplace. With a rapidly changing market, new competitors, and reduced cycle time, however, it is critical to reassess the company's unique and value-added role on a regular basis.

3. *Identifying the company's market niche.* The Strategic Alignment Method also ensures that the company is in the right business, is focused on the right market niche, and is able to identify and leverage its competitive advantage. This requires a substantial amount of data collection and analysis and, above all, the willingness to look at the business and be honest about its market position.

4. *Increasing the stakeholders' sense of ownership.* All the key stakeholders must be engaged in an up-front dialogue about the strategic direction of the business. The Strategic Alignment Method allows them to participate, gain new knowledge, develop respect and loyalty for what the organization is trying to do, build value, and eventually feel some degree of ownership for the results of the process. Without meaningful involvement, this value is never fully realized and the level of productive energy management can tap into is reduced.

The Elements of the Method

The steps of the Strategic Alignment Method used by Stahlcote are illustrated in Figures 5–1 and 5–2. There are two major phases: (1) ownership and alignment and (2) implementation.

Phase I: Ownership and Alignment

Phase I represents up-front planning with a long-term focus. It is a comprehensive review, focusing on where the organization is,

(*Text continues on page 94.*)

Figure 5-1. The Strategic Alignment Method, Phase I: Ownership and Alignment.

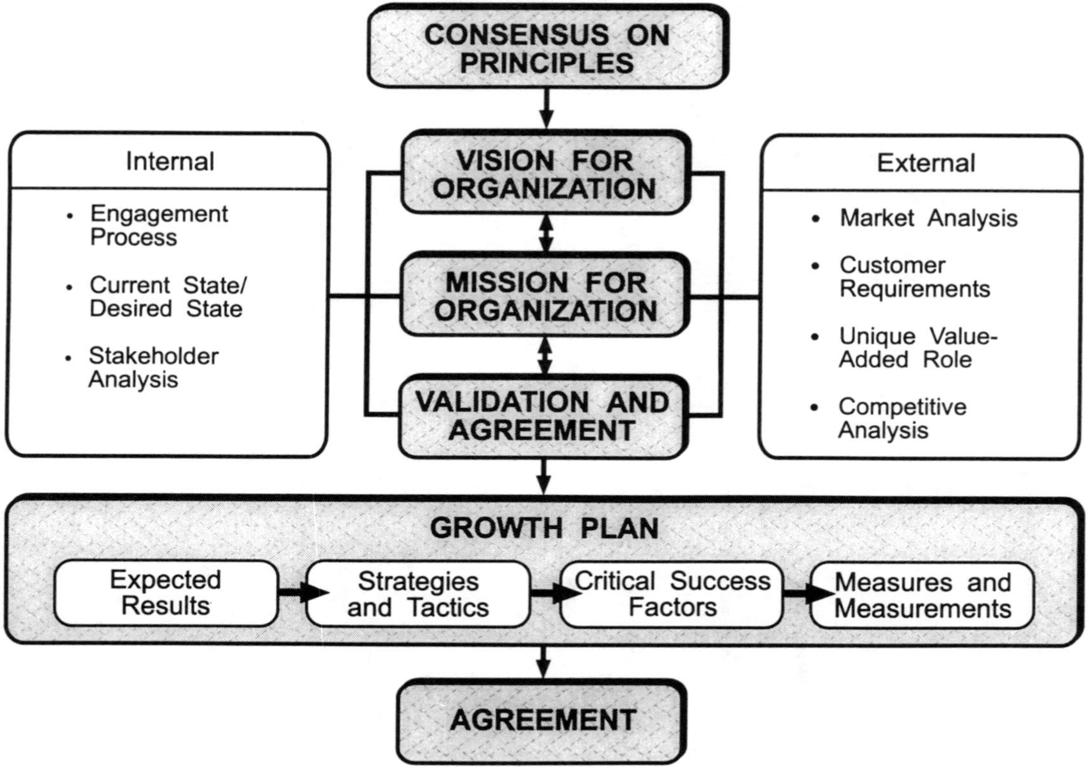

Figure 5–2. The Strategic Alignment Method, Phase II: Implementation.

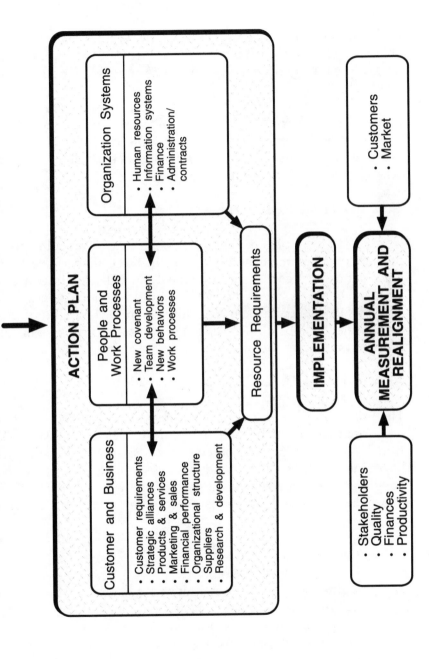

where it ought to be going, and how it will achieve its growth objectives. The key elements are: consensus on principles; vision for the organization; organization mission; validation and agreement; and the growth plan.

It cannot be emphasized enough how important it is to get fundamental agreement at each step in the process. Without it, the likelihood of disconnects from one or more members of the team increases. Fundamental agreement means an explicit, up-front decision, which in turn becomes a platform for the next step.

Consensus on Principles

In most strategic planning processes, agreement on principles is presumed rather than made explicit. In the Collaborative Workplace, an explicit consensus agreement about basic principles enables the business to weather difficult times. Stahlcote's principles were to value its people, be its customers' first choice, build trust-based relationships throughout the organizational system, and provide world-class-quality products and services.

Vision for the Organization

The purpose of the organization vision is to articulate what the organization wants to become in the future. What does the market want? What do the stakeholders want? For example, you might begin the process by answering this question: How does the company want to be known in the year 2000 or 2010? What will its reputation be? These questions need to be answered for each of the following:

1. Business and customer focus
2. Products and services offered
3. Culture and work environment
4. Leadership and management
5. People and work processes
6. Organization structure and systems

Visioning the organization occurs in several steps, in which the key leadership and a cross section of members from all parts and levels of the organization come together to articulate a three- to five-year vision. It was not long ago that we used to have a ten-year life span for a vision, but now, with the rapid rate of change, a shorter time frame is more realistic.

Step 1: Assessing the Current State

In each of the six areas listed above, the team generates as much data as it can about where the organization is at this juncture in its history. For example, the company may be focused on a specific niche market, be organized as a hierarchy, and have a compensation system based on individual competition. In the current-state assessment process, formal and hidden culture are both described. Figure 5–3 shows what the planning team at Stahlcote found. The team was truly astonished when they discovered the fundamental disconnect between the formal and hidden cultures. They proceeded to verify and validate their findings on up the line to the CEO. The accuracy of the team's assessment was borne out in what became a shared view. As the team pressed on through the analysis, they also found disconnects in the company's failure to produce results, its less-than-high-quality reputation in the industry, and its lack of alignment throughout its ranks.

Step 2: Creating the Desired State

The desired state is not simply the opposite of the current state. In this process, team members are emboldened to be creative, to stretch, to get outside the "nine dots," to think and dream big. This process is about developing a high level of ownership among team members regarding the future direction of the business.

At Stahlcote, the team had difficulty spelling out a vision beyond three years, so they brought in a futurist to talk about expected trends. They also benchmarked other companies to see what the best practices were and then decided to leapfrog them—to exceed even the best practices. By the time the team was through with the process, its members were able to look back in amazement at having been so ready to give up so early in the process.

Figure 5-3. Current-state work environment.

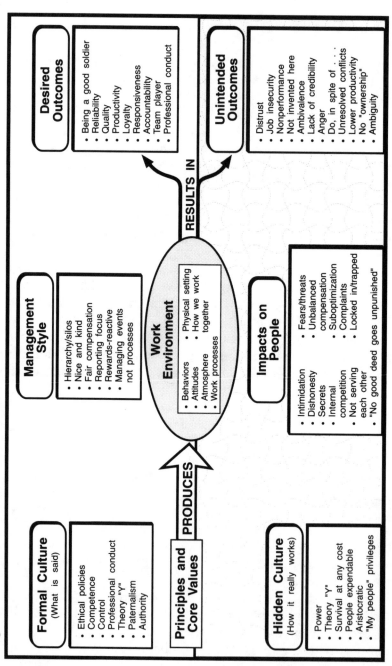

Formal Culture
(What is said)

- Ethical policies
- Competence
- Control
- Professional conduct
- Theory "Y"
- Paternalism
- Authority

Management Style

- Hierarchy/silos
- Nice and kind
- Fair compensation
- Reporting focus
- Rewards-reactive
- Managing events not processes

Desired Outcomes

- Being a good soldier
- Reliability
- Quality
- Productivity
- Loyalty
- Responsiveness
- Accountability
- Team player
- Professional conduct

Principles and Core Values

PRODUCES

Work Environment

- Behaviors
- Attitudes
- Atmosphere
- Work processes
- Physical setting
- How we work together

RESULTS IN

Hidden Culture
(How it really works)

- Power
- Theory "Y"
- Survival at any cost
- People expendable
- Aristocratic
- "My people" privileges

Impacts on People

- Intimidation
- Dishonesty
- Secrets
- Internal competition
- Not serving each other
- "No good deed goes unpunished"
- Fears/threats
- Unbalanced compensation
- Suboptimization
- Complaints
- Locked in/trapped

Unintended Outcomes

- Distrust
- Job insecurity
- Nonperformance
- Not invented here
- Ambivalence
- Lack of credibility
- Anger
- Do, in spite of . . .
- Unresolved conflicts
- Lower productivity
- No "ownership"
- Ambiguity

Step 3: Engaging the Organization and Validating the Draft Vision

Once the draft vision has been developed, everyone in the organization can be engaged at some level in understanding what it is and what it means for each individual. A focus-group process can be used to generate alignment and build value for the new direction. By the time Stahlcote's initial validation process had been completed, for example, the draft vision was as follows: To become the premier provider of laser-coated sheet metals in the world by the year 2010.

Mission for the Organization

Organization mission statements are sometimes confused with vision statements. In fact, some organizations transpose them. What, then, should the mission statement focus on? Why we are here? or What do we want the organization to become? Organizational direction? or simply Customer satisfaction?

In a Collaborative Workplace, the organization's mission statement defines who the company is. In one succinct statement, it answers three sets of questions:

1. Who are we? What is our identity? What business are we really in?
2. Who do we serve? Who are our customers/clients? What are their needs/requirements? What are they trying to do that requires our services/products?
3. What do we do? What are our services and products? What is the market?

A fourth question can also be asked: What do we intend to become? This question is often also addressed in the visioning process.

Developing the mission takes place in three distinct steps: drafting; external analysis; and internal analysis.

Step 1: Drafting the Mission Statement

Without the aid of any data, the team members begin by drafting a mission statement more or less off the top of their heads. They use a blank-sheet process to take a first crack at defining what the company is all about. It is cornerstone and foundation work. Sometimes the process is viewed as just another boring team development game or a diversion and gets trivialized. As more than one team member has said in this process: "When do I get to go back and do some real work?" But there is probably no more important work than understanding and agreeing on the mission of your organization and building value and ownership for it. Now comes the hard part—opening up the organization to a basic critique about its market niche, customer satisfaction, and the issue of whether the needs of the stakeholders are being met.

Step 2: Seeking External Analysis

The purpose of the external analysis is to truly understand the organization's unique and value-added role. Basic market research in the company's line of business will generate critical data on where the trends exist for the industry segment and product/service focus. Then, by engaging current and past customers in a serious dialogue about the company's value-added service and their own future requirements, cross-validating information can be obtained on where the market niche is. This process may result in some defensiveness, as perceptions of value are voiced. Sometimes it results in denial. Keeping an open mind is essential if this process is to work.

The third part of this analysis is developing a crystal clear statement of the company's unique and value-added role. What is it that truly makes the company distinctive in the marketplace? What specific value does it add, to whom, and with what results? While market and customer data inform this definition, it takes considerable discussion inside an organization among its key advisors to produce a succinct, one-sentence statement, such as: "Our unique and value-added role is that we have the only patented process in the world to produce synthetic skin."

The fourth part of the external analysis is to conduct research on the company's competitors—to understand who they are, what they do, how they present themselves, and how they are going after business. How do they distinguish themselves from your company and their other competitors? Once these data have been summarized and objectively analyzed, the strategic alignment team goes to work defining the company's competitive advantage in the marketplace. What specifically differentiates it from other companies? How is the company positioned relative to its competitors? What are its key features, and what are the benefits that accrue to potential customers from buying and using these services/products?

Step 3: Seeking Internal Analysis

Stahlcote knew that it had to redirect its market focus. It also knew that its employees wanted to have a voice in the process. With a high degree of urgency, its leadership launched an exhaustive series of strategic-thinking meetings with small focus groups across the company. At first, the employees appreciated being asked. "This new operations guy really means business. We're really going to be consulted this time." Energy went up—at least until the first draft of the vision and mission statement were released. Unfortunately, the draft did not reflect many of the key messages the workforce had given management. In the second draft, none of their suggested changes had been made. Needless to say, the skeptics who had thought that management had a hidden agenda were making the rounds with "I told you so," and a sense of resignation settled in. Obviously, it simply did not pay to participate.

A middle manager I know once referred to this approach to engagement as *participative management*, or "we participate, they manage." People are asked for their opinions, but the real purpose is co-optation, not an authentic interest in making substantive changes in what are predetermined results.

There *are* other ways to achieve a positive result. The collaborative process lays the foundation by building alignment and ownership for the mission. By creating an open engagement process, leadership can integrate the experience, expertise, and energy of the membership in crafting a statement that will have meaning and value to them.

Another part of the internal analysis is a systematic review of other stakeholders' interests and issues concerning the company's direction. A *stakeholder* is anyone with a sufficient stake in the organization or whose support you cannot do without. Engage stakeholders directly, but at the appropriate level. As a result of the alignment process, the organization mission for Stahlcote was: "We are a collaborative team totally dedicated to providing our customers with world-class precision products that can give them a competitive edge."

Validation, Upgrade, and Agreement

The credibility of the company's new direction will depend on the extent to which the key players agree at this stage. Focus groups, document upgrades, and final drafts help people see that their views matter. Changes can be made in the final document. When finished, the document can then be published to validate the stakeholders' views and continue to build ownership. As a result of the validation process at Stahlcote, the company's vision was changed slightly to reflect the increasing competition in the marketplace for laser-coated sheet metals, and the year was advanced to 2020. This put less pressure on the company's workforce to double the company's growth every year.

The Growth Plan

Prepare a growth plan which will allow the organization to move from vision to action. The growth plan is the bridge between theory and practice, between blue sky and reality. There are several elements: expected results; growth concept; strategies and tactics; critical success factors; and measures and measurement.

Spelling Out the Expected Results

The first part of the growth plan spells out the *expected results* for the next three years. A key distinction needs to be made here.

How many times have you heard someone say, "My goal/objective is to ... ," or "I intend to ... ," or "I hope to ..."? Then what happens? Often nothing. The roads to both Heaven and Hell are paved with good intentions, it is said, but St. Peter will admit only those who produce results. One of the best ways to make the expected results process real is to say "We will ..." and quantify the specific things to be accomplished by when and by whom.

At Stahlcote, specific revenue results were forecast for each quarter. Rather than glibly picking a number out of the sky, the group was expected to provide documentation on how those results would be achieved. At the end of the quarter, there was a review of what had or had not been produced, and the lessons learned were incorporated into the next quarter's process.

People generally resist setting quantitative targets, especially in an hierarchical culture. It makes them commit, and then they can be held accountable. *Stretch results* are even more threatening because they require us to put aside our assumptions about how things work and dig deep for a new level of commitment to achieve them. It requires people to step beyond the conventional wisdom of "we've always done it this way," and become creative—to risk and find new ways of thinking about stale subjects. The stretch result at Stahlcote was a 150 percent growth rate for each of the next five years, increasing market share from 5 to 20 percent by 2005.

Using a Growth Concept to Position the Company

The second element of the growth plan translates the expected results into a specific *growth concept* designed to position the company so that it can realize them. *Positioning* means that the company's competitive advantage will be advanced, its unique and value-added role will be maximized, and its attributes and benefits will be communicated to the market. Positioning means ensuring that the company is seen as truly distinctive in the market and entering it in a way that it can realize its full potential. Positioning also requires addressing any and all barriers to the company's growth. To achieve its stretch results, Stahlcote decided to position itself as the vendor of choice to 50 percent of the sheet metal purchasers from the Atlantic to the Mississippi (who represented

80 percent of all sheet metal consumption). What would its strategy be?

Developing a Specific Set of Strategies

The third element of the growth plan is to develop a specific set of *strategies* that will mobilize the organization's resources to produce the expected results. One Stahlcote strategy was to wage a public relations blitz to establish in the minds of its prospective customers an image of Stahlcote as the supplier with the most advanced thinking in the business. The campaign emphasized that Stahlcote was customer-focused and able to underprice the competition while producing world-class quality.

Identifying Barriers to Success

The fourth element in the growth plan is identifying the *barriers to the success of* the company's strategies. Barriers may exist in a wide variety of areas, ranging from a resistant workforce or an unreceptive culture to quality-assurance problems on the assembly line. Usually technical barriers can be resolved much more easily than attitudinal, cultural, or behavioral barriers. When, for example, the shop foreman at Stahlcote's finishing mill thought the new involvement process was really an attempt to undermine his position and authority, he managed to slow down the process without appearing to be in opposition to it.

Turning Barriers Into Success Factors

Once all the barriers have been identified, the next step is to turn them into *critical success factors*—those things that absolutely must happen if the effort is to be successful (e.g., when jumping from an airplane, you must have a parachute that opens). In the Stahlcote case of the resistant shop foreman, the strategy was to assure him that no jobs would be eliminated without active participation from the shop. A new strategic role was carved out for the workforce.

Creating a Set of Measures

The final element of the growth plan is a set of *measures* that allow the company to evaluate its progress over time and a *measurement process* that fully involves the workforce in understanding where they are and how they will make improvements. The measurement process should be focused on learning rather than on finding fault. The current paradigm often uses measures and measurement as a way of saying "You don't measure up"—an approach that tends to dampen enthusiasm for measurement. In fact, the paradox of the recent benchmarking fad is that it establishes as the highest standard the experience base of companies that have taken the last five to ten years to achieve it. In effect, enormous sums of money, time, and expert resources are invested in benchmarking the past rather than projecting a pathway to the future.

In the Collaborative Workplace, measures should be both quantitative and qualitative, informed by the past, but anticipating customer requirements in the future. By vectoring in on their requirements, the company can leapfrog the competition rather than constantly play catch-up.

Agreement

The team driving this process should pause at this juncture and make sure that the key stakeholders agree with the growth plan and are prepared to move toward implementation. If not, the team needs to identify the disconnects and upgrade the document until there is consensus.

Phase II: Implementation

The Stahlcote team was now ready to go. It had identified its new niche in the marketplace and developed a very high level of buy-in from across the organization about the new direction of the business. The company had invested heavily in developing the growth plan, and everyone had fundamentally agreed to the new strategy. Now the team members identified the specific actions they would take to achieve the expected results. Once the action plan was completed, they would identify their resource requirements, determine how they would manage the ongoing process of implementation, and decide how they would measure themselves annually.

The Action Plan

The Stahlcote team knew that there were three arenas for action planning: business and the customer; people and work processes; and organization systems. (See Figure 5–2.) The team members took each one of the expected results and strategies in the growth plan and mapped out who really needed to be involved in each part of the work. They went back to the stakeholder analysis as a checkpoint to make sure that they were involving the right people at the right time. Then they prioritized them in terms of achieving the expected results.

But before the team launched into this next phase of the program, it focused on achieving two immediate, high-visibility successes to generate a companywide sense of confidence and momentum. The team knew that what was needed to establish its overall credibility after all this planning, it needed a "quick hit" that could be directly attributed to the strategic alignment process—something tangible, visible, and significant to as many people in the organization as possible. The team identified one such potential success as the redesign of the career development program. It had been a thorn in the company's side for some time because it continued to reward individual accomplishment even though everyone in the organization was now working in teams. A second early success was identified as getting the workforce on-line and trained in the use of their multimillion-dollar electronic-mail system so that everyone could communicate with everyone else at will.

Arena 1: Business and Customers

Meanwhile, the team had identified the action steps that were needed in at least eight areas of the business and customer arena:

1. *Customer requirements and relationships.* The first priority was a new focus on the company's customers, building full-value contracts with each one. The team would initiate an engagement process, listen to the customers' requirements, work through process issues, and develop a new set of agreements. Team members chose a focus on the quality of the company's products and services. They established an aggressive standard to which they would reduce the error rate in their manufacturing process, increase response time to customer service requests, and shift the attitudes of Stahlcote members toward their customers.

2. *Strategic alliances.* With its new strategic alliance partners, Stahlcote needed to build a bridge to support the business and management requirements of the two companies. The team knew that the two organizations' corporate styles were really quite different; in fact, they were so different that the alliance was in danger of failing. The team recognized the need to build trust by creating a set of Operating Agreements, and a charter to govern their relationship.

3. *Products and services.* Given the new market niche, the current products and services of Stahlcote would no longer fit the bill. The team decided that they must be tailored to meet new customer requirements. Packaging would need to be different, and the customer follow-up service would have to be significantly upgraded to become proactive rather than reactive.

4. *Marketing and sales.* Even the traditional approach to the marketing and selling of Stahlcote products and services needed to be changed. The new focus would be on relationship selling. A different kind of sales force would be hired since new skills were needed. New information systems software would be installed to accommodate new data requirements.

5. *Financial performance.* Financial performance would still be a bottom-line indicator of success, but the new organization direction needed new measures, a different reporting process, a shift from cost centers to customer centers, and a supply chain attitude toward internal customers by the members of the finance, audit, and tax organizations.

6. *Organizational structure.* The basic structure had already shifted to collaborative teams. The leadership function would be

redefined and new roles and responsibilities would be spelled out.

7. *Suppliers.* Suppliers that had traditionally been pitted against each other needed to be recast as allies in the effort to achieve competitive advantage. The number of suppliers would be streamlined, full-value agreements would be negotiated, and a new type of relationship would be put in place to engender higher quality, lower cost, and more trust.

8. *Research and development.* New product development opportunities needed to be aligned with customers' requirements rather than simply being based on what was interesting to the scientists and engineers. R&D would become a full partner in the process of meeting customer requirements.

Arena 2: People and Work Processes

The Stahlcote team members identified specific actions that would be needed in five key areas:

1. *A new covenant.* The company needed to create a new covenant that would clarify the mutual expectations and responsibilities of its managers and employees. Part of that covenant would be the principles that would guide their behavior. The new covenant would talk about loyalty and commitment in the context of a changing market. It would provide a cultural framework for internal work processes and systems that would build ownership and alignment across the enterprise. Finally, the covenant would consider the obligations of the business to its members should the company fall on hard times. If layoffs were needed, the document would spell out how they would be handled. In effect, the normally secret or confidential aspects of business management would be opened up.

2. *Team development.* The team wanted a Collaborative Workplace, but it knew that culture cannot just be changed as a function of business strategy. Cultural change is the result of many other action-forcing events and activities. The team members decided to create the new culture by establishing functional teams, project teams, and cross-functional teams throughout Stahlcote. Each team would use the collaborative team formation process, and

gradually the new culture would show up in new behaviors and work processes.

3. *New behaviors.* Each team would establish its own Operating Agreements, charter, and work program aligned with the company's strategic direction. The change team knew that it would be difficult to alter old habits, so it built into the process skills development, a buddy system, and a coaching process to ensure success.

4. *Core competencies.* The team took aim at the new skill requirements of the business. No longer would the hiring requirements be based on internally focused criteria. From now on, the focus would be on the skills needed to meet customer requirements and on the ability to function in a more collaborative, fluid work environment. No longer would the company use the traditional processes of recruitment at engineering schools, screening applicants on the basis of degrees and technical skills. It would reposition itself as an industry leader and thus offer the applicants a challenging career into the 21st century if they performed well. A profile of the successful candidate would have to be developed, and a targeted recruitment strategy developed. Because jobs were no longer "for life," the risk profile and flexibility quotient of the candidates had to be very high. The team members felt it was essential to their integrity to put this profile up-front in the process.

5. *Work processes.* Business processes would need to be redesigned, but they would be implemented in an entirely different way than in the past. Stahlcote decided that it would launch changes in this area only after it had workforce buy-in to the new strategic direction of the company and after it had put in place a cadre of trained leaders who could facilitate the process. The company recognized that the expertise on what needed to be fixed lay with the existing workforce. The team knew that threatening job security was not the way to win their loyalty or build value for the change. Therefore, it was decided that those affected by the change would participate in the redesign process.

Arena 3: Organization Systems

The team was ready to move on. One major issue remained to be addressed: the four major organizational systems that made up the infrastructure of the company. The team decided to make the actual behaviors and design of these support systems congruent with the core values of the Collaborative Workplace, recognizing that this would represent a big change for systems people, most of whom were more focused on their jobs than on the customer.

• *Human resources.* Perhaps the greatest changes would have to occur in human resources, where the focus had been on hiring, firing, performance appraisals, and benefits administration. In the new Stahlcote, this division would become a change agent and provide skills development. Because the organization was much flatter, with only four levels rather than 15, the performance appraisal system would need redesigning to reflect the new role of teams. The forced ranking system would be replaced by 360-degree feedback and a more interactive learning process between managers and members. The concept of advancement would also require redefinition since the career ladder had disappeared.

The Stahlcote team also decided to reduce the size of the central HR staff, placing its people out in the business units and on cross-functional customer-focused teams. The shift to a collaborative organization would also mean an entirely new skills-development effort integrated into the overall organization development of the company. There would need to be an emphasis on building self-sufficiency skills in key members to ensure the ongoing successful evolution of Stahlcote.

• *Information systems.* The team decided to put the information systems requirements for change at the end of the change effort. As part of the business process redesign effort, information requirements would be identified and put into the overall strategy for change. A conscious decision was made not to let information requirements drive business strategy.

• *Finance.* It was also decided to refocus the finance function on the customer. A customer-engagement process would be launched to begin building a new type of relationship with internal customers. New agreements would be reached, and financial reporting requirements would be redesigned to focus on customer requirements.

- *Administration and legal.* This group also needed to go through a customer-engagement process to establish a new type of work relationship with their internal customers. New standards for service delivery would be developed, and they would focus on building a can-do reputation.

Resource Requirements

The Stahlcote action plan had a section on the resources it would require to implement the plan:

- *New people and skill competencies.* Different types of people would be needed at Stahlcote, and the process required to find them would need to be repositioned. This would take time, money, and new leadership. Executives would need to be involved in hiring.
- *Loyalty and commitment.* Top management would need to remain committed to the action plan, even in the face of resistance and economic difficulties. Throughout the company there would need to be an increased level of loyalty and commitment to the new direction.
- *Productivity levels.* The team knew that, starting with a productivity level of about 35 percent, the company would need to make an investment in skills development, team formation, and alignment to ensure that the engagement process was in full swing. To justify the investment, the expected result was a 200 percent increase in productivity.
- *Equipment and material.* The company would also need to invest in new equipment, software, and networking to ensure that the members were directly communicating with each other, their customers, and their suppliers.
- *Finances.* All these actions would require additional capital, which would be built into the budget and amortized over five years. The team projected that cost savings and productivity increases would begin producing on the bottom line within two years.

Implementation, Measurement, and Realignment

Before the Stahlcote team implemented the plan, it once again engaged the key stakeholders in the agreement process, which was upgraded and then rolled out to the entire organization. Now the hard part began. Stahlcote members had to begin changing their behaviors. Everyone had to take more responsibility for the business.

Implementation is a critical challenge facing the Collaborative Workplace. Everyone must be involved at some level, and everyone must feel responsible for the success of the enterprise. Members who were once employees can no longer sit back and simply do what they are told. Managers who were once bosses can no longer simply use their authority to order people around. The entire character of the work relationship must change, becoming much more mutual and more focused on meeting customer requirements, building value, achieving expected results, and collaboratively solving problems.

Key to finding solutions is the creation of a comprehensive system of measures and measurement to ensure that all members of the company know where they stand. Measures must be established for every aspect of the organization's operations, customers, and culture.

Accountability processes must also be installed so that members can learn and grow from their mistakes. Periodic evaluation throughout the organization produces data that will allow all concerned to make the necessary adjustments to systems or work processes. In addition, a renewal process should be launched every year to ensure that the organization remains strategically aligned. There can be no standing still if the business expects to remain competitive.

Summary

Most companies are in a *reactive mode*. They are reacting to their competitors, the new realities of the workplace, and the latest programs to transform their businesses. When they decide to realign their businesses, it is usually done from the top down and nearly always involves some structural change. Even the strategic planning process is ordered from the top without much buy-in or involvement from the workforce. As we have seen, without that buy-in, ownership, and involvement, true alignment is not possible. The Collaborative Workplace uses the Strategic Alignment Method to build value for the new business direction among all stakeholders, focusing the business on the customer, and re-aligning the culture and critical work processes. No stone is left unturned, and the business is not left in a position where it can be run over.

6

Collaborative Teams

All for one, one for all, . . .
—D'Artagnon in Dumas,
The Three Musketeers

More and more, businesses are migrating from committees and departmental-based task groups to teams and team-based organizations. Whether they are self-directed, high-performance, autonomous, or empowered teams, their work processes are basically the same. They are usually given a set of tasks to accomplish, and when they begin, they start with the traditional team process of forming and norming. It is usually not long before the members start storming. The power games of the committee have merely been transferred to the team environment. Often it is not long before team members lose confidence in the process and enthusiasm begins to wane. Gradually business leaders are learning that just because you call a group of people a "team" does not necessarily mean they are one.

This chapter describes the use of collaborative teams as the basic work unit of the Collaborative Workplace—a structure that can fulfill the promise of empowerment with accountability. This chapter also considers a process for managing these teams for success and suggests the types of documents needed to govern them.

The Team-Based Structure of a Collaborative Workplace

As a structure, the new workplace is managed by teams that are founded on the core values of collaboration. The organization is

Figure 6–1. The team structure of a Collaborative Workplace.

internally aligned, operates with integrity, and as a business meets the strategic needs of its stakeholders.

The structure is flat. The symbol for this workplace is the circle, which represents unity, equality, and mutual respect. It is ideally suited for a networked company or any organization that requires high levels of trust, accountability, and responsibility among its members. (See Figure 6–1.)

In this structure, there are at least three levels of collaborative teams: strategic, tactical, and operational:

1. *Strategic.* Leadership or even functional teams provide overall guidance and direction to the organization on its vision, mission, key strategies, and/or specific functions or tasks. Consensus decision making is essential at this level.

2. *Tactical.* Collaborative teams focus on how the vision, mission, and strategies/tasks will be achieved within a given set of boundaries or parameters. Consensus decision making is highly valued but not absolutely essential at this level.

3. *Operational.* Collaborative teams or natural work groups implement the strategies and tactics. They have wide autonomy in the implementation process as long as their actions are aligned with the strategic direction of the business.

Some collaborative teams may operate on all three levels. In practice the strategic leadership team is usually populated with more experienced members and tends not to become involved in the tactical work. There should be a one- or two-person overlap between strategic and tactical teams and between tactical and operational teams. This is essential to ensure that there are no communication disconnects between the two groups, that they remain aligned, have a shared view about what they are supposed to be doing, and build value for the expected results.

Creating Collaborative Teams

The purpose of creating collaborative teams is to build ownership of the team's operations and to ensure the alignment of its members with the strategic direction of the company. It is a major, upfront process that engages the members in an in-depth conversation about why they are there, who they are, how they will work together, what they are going to do when, and how they will measure their success. There are eight steps in what will be called the collaborative team formation process. (See Figure 6–2.)

Step 1: Clarifying the Team's Task or Function

Most teams are formed with a specific purpose in mind. Regardless of the task or time frame, it is critical at the outset that the team absolutely understand what is expected of it and that every member share that same understanding. It is best if this task clari-

Figure 6–2. Creating collaborative teams.

	Team Formation Process	Team Management Process	Self-Sufficiency	Self-Renewal	Team Closing Process
C O M M I T M E N T A S S E S S M E N T	• Team Task/ Function	• Planning Implementation	• Self-Sufficiency Skills	• Assessment	• Review
	• Roles and Responsibilities	• Business Strategy	• Training the Leaders	• Blank Sheet Re-visioning	• Recognition
	• Operating Agreements	• Group Dynamics	• Measurement	• Recommitment	• Learning
	• Chartering	• Issues Management			• Sunset
	• Critical Success Factors	• Skills Management			
	• Action Plan	• Measurement			
	• Skills Development				
	• Measurement				

↓   A ↓ **Learning** ↓ **Oganization** ↓

RESULTS: (Quality) (Service) (Profit) (Empowerment)

fication is done with the sponsor to ensure alignment of purpose, outcomes, and process. In team after team, a major disconnect occurs when there is a difference of perspective between the team members and the sponsor assigning the task. We have to be very careful here, because in a hierarchical work system that is trying to become collaborative, there is a reluctance to challenge or question someone higher up in authority. But when the team is well down the road, those questions always emerge and can become a wedge between the sponsor and the team, resulting in mutual distrust and/or a lower-quality product.

Step 2: Clarifying Team Roles and Responsibilities

In Chapter 4, we identified seven roles to be played by leaders and members of a team: sponsor, facilitator, coach/mentor, change agent/catalyst, healer, member, and manager/administrator.

Right from the outset of the team formation process, it is fundamental that everyone know and understand who is playing what
role and when, since roles and responsibilities will change over
time. All too often, teams begin their work with unspoken assumptions about who is supposed to do what. In a hierarchical work
environment, there is the added dilemma of who the leader is—
since position, title, and authority are usually synonymous. A clear
statement and clarification up-front about the leadership function,
the different roles, and how the team can take responsibility for
performing those roles from time to time is essential for effective
group dynamics.

Step 3: Establishing Operating Agreements

This process, which has been fully discussed in Chapter 3, occurs
immediately after the task and roles have been clarified.

Step 4: Creating a Team Charter

A charter is a formal governance document that represents the
purpose of the team in relation to the organization, who its members are, and how they will work together. This document spells
out the team's vision and mission, the benefits of fulfilling that
mission excellently, its key strategies and critical success factors,
quality standards, boundary conditions, and Operating Agreements. A sample collaborative team charter may be found in Figure 6–3. The chartering process operates by true consensus and
produces alignment among all team members. When there are
more than two teams in an organization, it is important that all
team charters be rationalized to avoid overlap or duplication. This
process also enhances alignment and clarifies team roles and responsibilities.

Step 5: Identifying Critical Success Factors

The critical success factors represent those achievements, characteristics, and/or processes that absolutely must happen for the
team to be considered successful in implementing its charter.

Figure 6–3. Sample team charter.

Mission

As valued and empowered people, we shall continuously enhance our partners' competitive position by providing high-quality, cost-effective information systems and services.

KEY PURSUITS

Satisfy customer information needs
- Maintain and enhance our existing materials maintenance and administrative service systems
- Maintain an acceptable level of responsiveness to customer requests
- Meet or exceed customer expectations

Seek ways to continuously improve the quality and cost-effectiveness of our systems
- Eliminate rework by doing the job right the first time
- Incorporate established standards in our systems development
- Stay abreast of technology when it makes sense
- Do our job at the lowest possible cost without sacrificing the other key pursuits

Promote professional excellence
- Provide professional development training
- Offer on-the-job development opportunities
- Embrace collaborative teams

GUIDING PRINCIPLES AND CONCEPTS

- Value and empower our people
- Enhance our customers' competitive position
- Strive for "World Class" performance
- Align with corporate direction
- Work together as a team
- Make *best* business decisions instead of easiest, quickest, cheapest
- Expand benefits
- Collaborate with the planning team

BOUNDARIES

- Adhere to the established development budget (dollars and personnel)
- Develop, maintain, and support only company and related products
- Make development decisions in partnership with our customers
- Not assume responsibilities belonging to other teams
- Support and adhere to the charter

BENEFITS

External Partners
- Higher-quality product that is continuously improving
- Customer needs that are understood and met
- Improved customer satisfaction
- Lower cost of doing business
- Increased respect and credibility, because our customers' needs are met with such high quality
- Customer solutions that have broader base in knowledge, creativity, and innovation and faster, better decisions, because our decisions are made by a team
- Better ability to adapt to future needs

Internal Partners
- Increased respect and value for each member of the team
- Improved morale, job satisfaction, happiness
- More opportunities for innovative, creative input
- Enhanced relationships with management
- Shared responsibility with other teams
- More pride in our jobs
- Improved opportunity
- Better ability to stay abreast of new technology

Step 6: Developing an Action Plan

This action plan is different from the organization's strategic document discussed in Chapter 5. The scope of this plan includes what it will take for the team to achieve its vision and mission and produce its deliverables. It also includes a detailed road map for who does what when.

Step 7: Beginning Collaborative Skills Development

There is a basic set of collaborative skills that a team needs—what could be called basic blocking and tackling skills—so that everyone is operating on the same level of understanding about how collaborative team processes are supposed to work. These skills include collaborative meeting design and facilitation, collaborative problem solving, and action planning.

Step 8: Establishing Measures and Measuring Progress

How will the team know when it gets there? First by defining where "there" is; then by taking a measurement of where it begins; and finally by measuring its progress along the way. As we discussed in Chapter 5, measurement is essential to documenting successes, learning from mistakes, and growing the organization's shared knowledge about how best to serve the customer. Some typical measures collaborative teams use include: customer satisfaction, decision turnaround time, ownership in decisions, cycle time, bottom-line financial results, member satisfaction, and the quality of the workplace culture.

The Team Management Process

The procurement cross-functional team had done all the right things. It had completed the formation process right on schedule. It had reached true consensus on its Operating Agreements and charter. It knew what it had to do. The members were enthusiastic about their work. The sponsor was pleased with the quick liftoff, and confidence had soared. Within three months, however, some members started showing up late for meetings. Differences were more pronounced than in the early weeks. Value appeared to have been lost. The bulk of the workload began to fall on several members, and resentments began to grow. What had happened?

The short answer is that teams and team members grow, change, and often revert to old behaviors. The ongoing management of relationships is not something we have learned very well. Some possible explanations include the following:

- Team members begin to take each other for granted and assume that little has changed since day one.
- Someone on the periphery of the team decides that it should not continue its work and acts in a way that undercuts the team's purpose or credibility.
- Team members have not adequately processed their differences, leading to many unresolved issues.
- The Operating Agreements have not been kept, or there is a breach in integrity.
- Some team members may revert to old behavior because they may not want to change.
- Time constraints grow to a point where gridlock sets in, overloaded members rebel, and the team's priorities are undermined.

These types of breakdowns can be avoided by paying particular attention to four basic areas: people and group dynamics; business strategy; skills enhancement; and measurement.

People and Group Dynamics

The team needs to keep a close watch on the quality of work relationships, quickly identifying areas of conflict or disagreement and addressing them. Conflict avoidance, manipulation of the group process, and triangulation of differences are surefire ways to sabotage the team.

Another issue many teams face is problem members. While the Operating Agreements process will provide teams with preventions to address this concern, there are often individuals who decide, for various reasons, to continue to disrupt the process. These individuals may need coaching, counseling, or even administrative action.

New members joining the team can also divert productivity as members seek to bring the new participants up to speed. In the Collaborative Workplace, new members are introduced with great care, with preventions put in place before the member joins. These preventions include an agreement that they will behave in a manner consistent with the team's process. An orientation program is developed and, once on board, they are provided with a mentor/buddy who ensures that there is understanding and alignment along the way. Finally, new members are given ample opportunity to challenge and offer upgrades to the Operating Agreements, charter, and action plan. This builds value and ownership.

Business Strategy

During the course of a team's life, there will be significant changes in the organization's structure, leadership, strategic direction, customer base, or products and services. No matter how aligned the team is, these changes can have a significant impact on their dynamics—e.g., lost momentum or productivity as the team regroups; conflict over a new direction; or redirected energy if one or more team members leave. If there is a new sponsor, time will have to be spent bringing that person up to speed, after which the sponsor may refocus the direction of the team altogether.

These external changes need to be on the team's agenda. They offer the team an opportunity to apply the principle of collaboration to its business process, to use its Operating Agreements, to revisit its charter, and to develop a win-win course of action for the whole team.

Another possible scenario, especially for a team that is functioning well, is that it gets additional work assignments. This is yet another opportunity for the team to use its internal processes to realign, reassess, and recommit.

Skills Enhancement

As the team grows and changes, a crucial key to managing it for success is to increase each member's level of and proficiency in collaborative skills. This spreads the responsibility for the leadership function, increases confidence, and allows the team to mature. Among the skills that can be learned are: advanced collaborative team facilitation; strategic interventions and conflict resolution; and group and team dynamics. In effect, the company commits to an ongoing, just-in-time skills development process that continues to raise the bar of effectiveness and eventually leads to self-sufficiency.

Measures and Measurement

At set intervals during the life span of the team, the measures identified earlier should be applied. This helps prevent members from taking each other for granted, provides an objective perspective on the team's progress, and allows the team to make the appropriate management or process interventions to get the group back on track.

The Self-Sufficiency and Self-Renewal Process

Just as the organization will mature into a more self-sufficient entity, so too does each collaborative team, in a process that may take close to a year. Eventually a team reaches a point where its level of skill and effectiveness in leading and managing needs to be ratcheted up one more level—to that of self-sufficiency. By this time, the team will have several individuals who have demonstrated their ability and skill in handling its dynamics. These individual leaders understand organizational and change dynamics, have articulated their own management philosophies, and have played a process leadership role.

Since nothing remains static, the self-renewal process is equally important for the team. After about two years of working together on the basis of their original charter and Operating

Agreements, the team's focus can become stale. At this point, it needs to start all over again and reset the foundation of the team.

The Team Closing Process

When a team is successful—when its members have become a close working unit through the formation process and seen each other through the trials and tribulations of getting their product or work completed—it can be very hard to bring the association to a close. In many instances, however, they are required to, particularly in project-based organizations.

In keeping with the core values of the Collaborative Workplace, the process used to meet the emotional and psychological needs of team members is called *sunsetting*. This is a formal closing of the team and involves a number of critical components:

- A review of the achievements, outputs, and measurements for the team
- A review of the team's collaborative process, and what it took to make it work
- Recognition of each team member's responsibility and achievements in reaching those results
- An opportunity to review lessons learned at three levels: content, process, and culture
- An opportunity for members to acknowledge each other as individuals of value

In effect, sunsetting provides a sense of completion, fulfillment, and value and benchmarks the growth of the group. Each of the team's members can then leave feeling acknowledged, whole, and confident in his or her abilities to serve others using valuable new skills.

If for any reason the team breaks up before it completes its task or function, it is still critical to formally bring it to a close. This allows its members to grieve for the loss and plan for the future. They can then go on to other teams, where they will apply their experience, skills, and lessons learned.

Collaborative Team Documents

A collaborative team will generate a number of governance documents during its life span. These documents represent the identity of the team and provide a reminder as to what was agreed. They are also helpful in maintaining team focus on what it has accomplished. Often team members forget what they did or what they said six months before and make decisions that may not be consistent with their agreed-upon direction. Among the core documents that a team could expect to develop are:

People/Culture Documents

- Core values and principles
- Assessment of the current and desired states
- Workplace Culture Index, benchmark study
- Operating Agreements
- Team charter

Business/Customer Documents

- Vision and mission
- Strategic business direction
- Team and organization critical success factors
- Business growth plan
- Action/implementation plan
- Full-value contracts with customers

Business Process and Systems Documents

- Business process redesigns
- Human resource plan
- Information systems plan
- Finance and administration plans

Summary

Collaborative teams are the primary building block of the Collaborative Workplace. They give form and substance to the core values of collaboration. They provide a structure for the work to get done. They bring the workforce together to focus on real issues in real time, bringing real value to the bottom line. They bring the collaborative process to life, as members of the organization work through their issues in an accountable structure.

The team formation process ensures some degree of uniformity in building the Collaborative Workplace. As teams engage in the process, these members bring the new culture into being. The collaborative team management process allows the organization to mature, building a level of proficiency and confidence in how to handle the dynamics of a more responsible, accountable, and trusting workplace. The self-sufficiency, self-renewal, and closing processes merely punctuate a new level of self-reliance as the Collaborative Workplace takes on a life of its own.

Part II
The Collaborative Change Process

7

The Collaborative Method

*The important thing in life is to have a great aim and to possess the
aptitude and the perseverance to attain it.*
—*Johann Wolfgang von Goethe*

The senior staff members of the 1,500-member service company
were brimming with enthusiasm. They had just finished an extraordinary work session in which all 1,500 had helped develop
their new company vision. They simply could not stop talking
about how much it meant to them that everyone had this chance
to buy in. It was clear that this organization had high self-esteem.
You could feel the excitement in the air and sense the pride and
loyalty. You could see their energy and enthusiasm for their work
and their customers. This highly valued workforce was smiling,
eager to tell their story and to serve their customers. Their company is an example of a Collaborative Workplace. It is aligned and
engaged in discovering the power of the workplace culture in
achieving a competitive edge in the market.

Most of us do not work in places that are this alive, although
I suspect most of us would like to. How do we create this kind of
workplace? And once we have created such a workplace, how do
we sustain it over the long term?

This chapter explores a specific methodology that can be used
to create a Collaborative Workplace. Indeed, even the methodology itself is collaborative. First, we consider the power of the workplace culture as the primary vehicle for organizational change and
transformation and take a look at several alternative ways of im-

plementing change. Then we introduce the Collaborative Method, an analytic tool based on the premise that long-lasting change in any organization must begin with the culture.

The Power of the Workplace Culture

Much as we'd like to think so, energy, pride, loyalty, and a passion for work are not created by an organizational structure, a leader, a product, or a work process. They are all created by the people who work together every day in our organizations. These members of the workforce have dreams, hopes, and expectations. They have issues and problems. They have values, principles, and deeply held beliefs. They want to succeed and contribute. This is what I call the workplace culture, the place in people's hearts and minds where these dreams, concerns, and values play themselves out. The workplace culture is perhaps the least understood but most powerful force for organizational transformation in any enterprise. What is its power? How does it work? How do we engage it so that it drives the change process?

The Formal and Hidden Workplace Cultures

The task for Hi-Tech's cross-functional leadership team was to understand why the company was becoming increasingly noncompetitive. The team began its process by assessing the company's current state and then suggesting its desired state. The results astounded even the most optimistic members of the group. They found that work got done "in spite of management." They learned that there was a major difference between the formal workplace culture—those things that were said publicly about the company's values—and what might be called the *hidden workplace culture*—how the company really worked. (See Figure 7–1.) They realized that the gap between Hi-Tech's formal and hidden workplace cultures was responsible for the company's low level of productivity, which was at 30 percent. The team attributed this low level of effectiveness to the belief by the workforce that the company was "out of integrity"—i.e., that it was not living up to the values and beliefs it publicly espoused.

Figure 7–1. The hidden workplace culture: We work in two worlds.

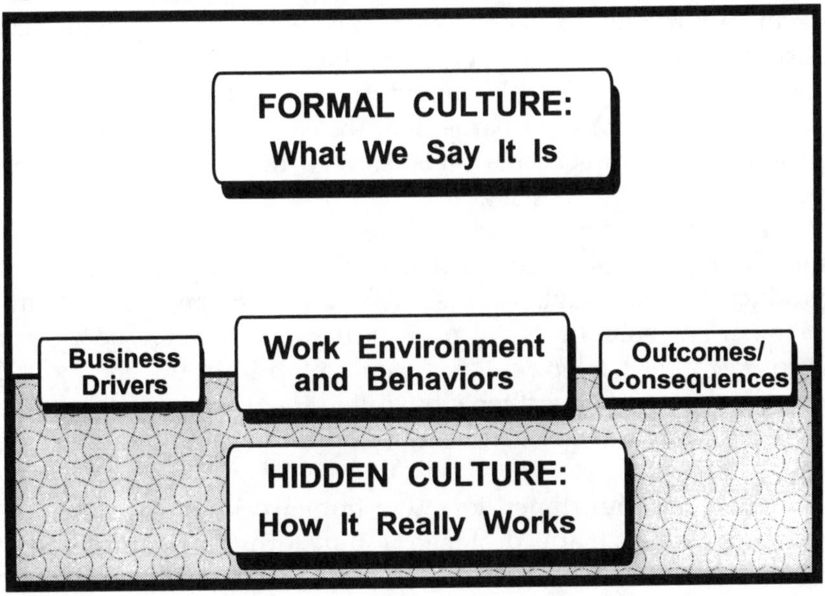

Fully 70 percent of the productive energy of the workforce was not available to meet the organization's strategic objectives. Even the available 30 percent was being threatened by the latest effort to make the company competitive—reengineering. More jobs were being lost as Hi-Tech continued down its slippery financial slope.

As we saw earlier, the hidden workplace culture is that place where people go in their minds and hearts when they do not feel valued or respected by their organization or when they do not feel ownership of the work processes. The hidden culture is where the real power and synergy of the company resides. Sometimes the spirit and enthusiasm of an entire company can get lost in this place when morale is low and skepticism is high.

One major index of the size and importance of the hidden workplace culture is called the *hidden productivity* of the workforce. Hidden productivity occurs when people withhold their energy, loyalty, and commitment from the organization because they do not feel valued or involved. It is ironic that, as companies look for ways to cut costs, they usually do not look at how to tap into this hidden productivity. It is real money being left on the table. In fact, having a partially productive workforce is the single biggest cost of doing business. When people feel their security is being threatened, productivity goes down and more costs have to be cut. It is a vicious cycle. Without harnessing that productivity to the company's strategic direction, it becomes very difficult to achieve competitive advantage. (See Figure 7–2.)

How do we tap into that hidden productivity? How can we unlock the energies and creativity of the workplace culture to produce breakthrough results, new behavior, and long-lasting change? The solution is *not* more structural change. The answer is to *engage the total workplace culture,* to tap in to the energy and commitment of the workforce by giving them a role in redefining how the work will get done and an opportunity to buy in to the change process.

There are four dimensions to a framework for implementing a change process that is designed to transform the organization: It can be *imposed on* the workforce by management, or the workforce can be *engaged in* the process. In most cases, the change process is initiated by management in reaction to changes in the marketplace. In a few instances, management will take a proactive posture by planning for the future. By cross-referencing these variables on a matrix, we can identify five different ways of leading a change effort. (See Figure 7–3.)

1. *Structure first.* The most common examples of the structure-first approach are reengineering/downsizing, reorganizing, and/or the decentralizing/recentralizing of key functions. The change effort is driven by events that have not been anticipated or planned, such as the urgency to reduce costs due to increasing competitive pressures. The company finds itself in a reactive mode, and the CEO and/or top management decide by themselves to impose the change to ensure the competitive viability of the company. There is little value placed on consulting with the workforce.

2. *Influence management.* In this approach, leadership has recognized the need for a change for some time. Financial performance and market research have consistently shown over the past

Figure 7-2. Hidden productivity before and after structural change.

UNUSED OR UNDERUTILIZED CAPACITY

100%

30-40%

0%

Workforce Productivity

Before Structural Change

After Structural Change

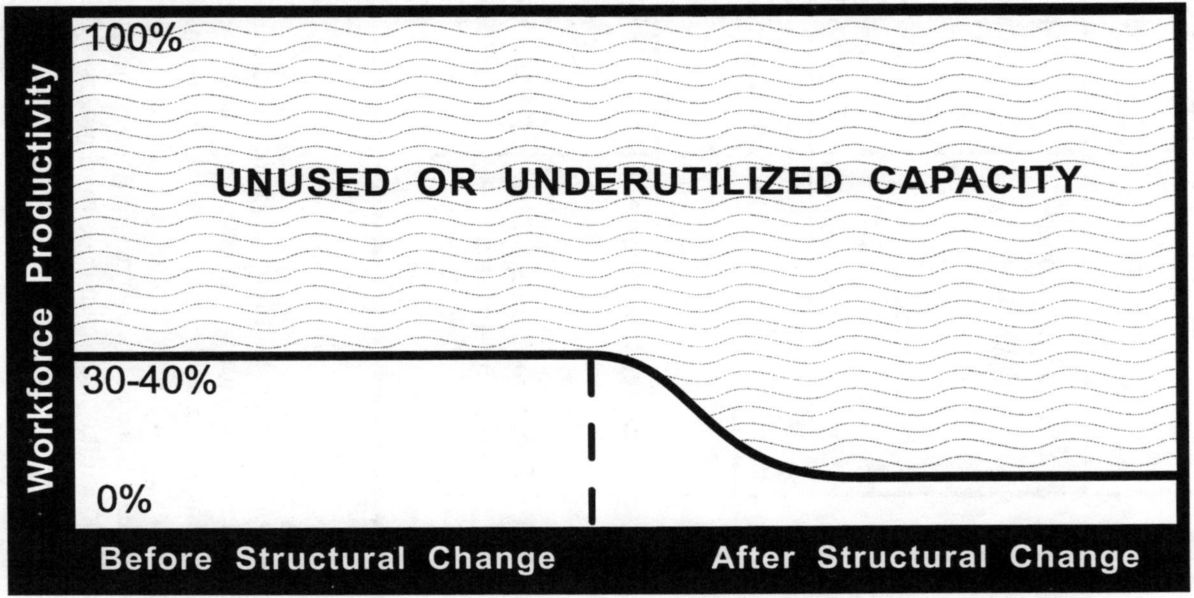

Figure 7–3. Alternative approaches to change.

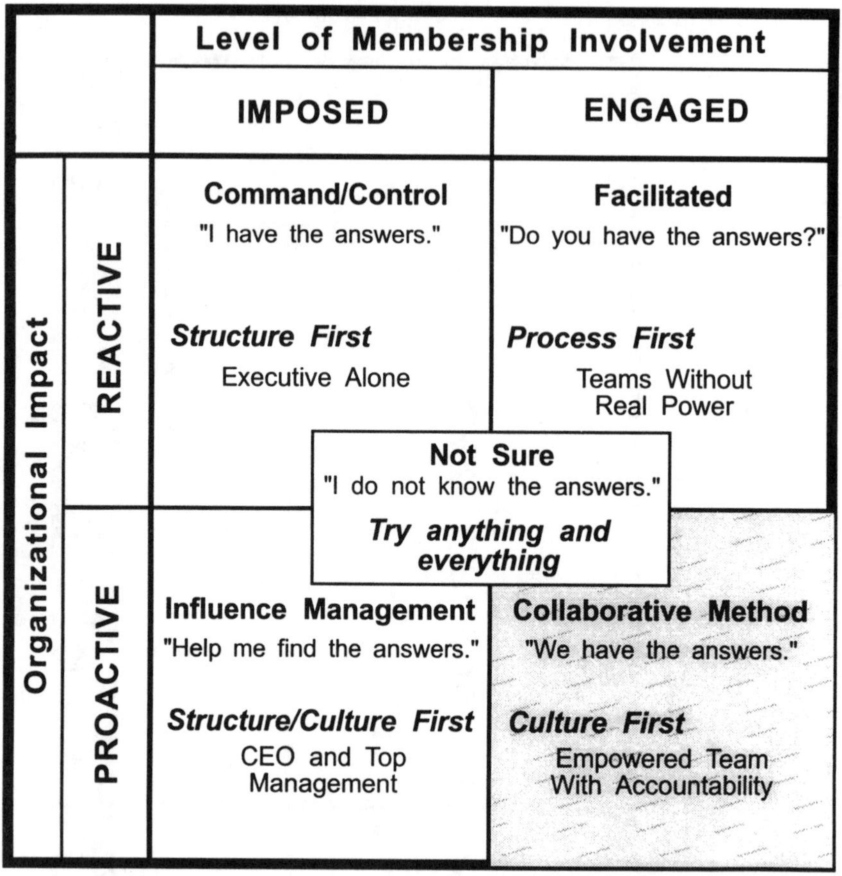

		Level of Membership Involvement	
		IMPOSED	**ENGAGED**
Organizational Impact	**REACTIVE**	**Command/Control** "I have the answers." *Structure First* Executive Alone	**Facilitated** "Do you have the answers?" *Process First* Teams Without Real Power
		Not Sure "I do not know the answers." *Try anything and everything*	
	PROACTIVE	**Influence Management** "Help me find the answers." *Structure/Culture First* CEO and Top Management	**Collaborative Method** "We have the answers." *Culture First* Empowered Team With Accountability

6 to 12 months that something needs to be done. A top leadership team is identified to advise the executive on the solution, and often a consulting company is hired. The executive reaches out to specific trusted individuals, looking for advice on the best course of action. The information is gathered from individuals, the team, and the consultant, and the executive makes a decision. Usually the decision is to impose a structural solution on the workforce, although there may also be process improvements.

   3. *Facilitated change.* This approach is often used when there

has been a crisis at the company, such as the loss of a major client or a substantial quarterly deficit that takes everyone by surprise. The executive wants the workforce involved in helping to solve the problem and creates several task teams that are chartered to make recommendations in key areas. The emphasis is on increased workforce participation through a process facilitated by internal or external resources. The teams complete their work and make their recommendations, but few if any are accepted. Some teams are told that they have given the wrong answers. In effect, just because there is more participation does not necessarily mean that the workforce actually has any influence.

4. *Try anything.* In some cases, the executives do not know what the solutions to the problems are and may say so. They will tend to try anything and everything to see if it will work. In this situation there is some likelihood that the solution will be seen as the program-of-the-month rather than a rational assessment of the problem. The level of involvement by the workforce may be high or low, but the solutions will most likely be imposed.

5. *Collaborative method.* The fifth option for management is the collaborative option—to be proactive in identifying issues and the need for a major organizational change and to engage the workforce in a process to determine the most appropriate response. The workforce builds value for the change and uses their knowledge of the business to implement the most effective changes.

The Collaborative Method: A Definition

The Collaborative Method is a change process that harnesses the values of collaboration to the power of the workplace culture to produce long-lasting change and breakthrough results for the enterprise. Based on the values of alignment, ownership, and full responsibility, the Collaborative Method uses a range of tools and processes to engage key stakeholders and ensure that the business is headed in the right direction, that the workforce has bought in, and that everyone takes responsibility for the success of the business.

Key Assumptions

There are a number of key assumptions that guide the successful application of the Collaborative Method to any change process, no matter how large or small.

• *Workforce involvement*. Leaders usually do not implement change. The workforce does. Therefore, they have a right and responsibility to be as directly involved as possible, from strategic alignment to implementation. Failure to involve them in a proactive, meaningful process merely increases the company's hidden productivity, and may even result in sabotage.

• *The circle, rather than the pyramid*. The circle is the symbol of the collaboration. It represents strength and unity. When contrasted with the hierarchical pyramid, the circle represents a sense of equality, common purpose, and shared views about what is important. A circle is one of the strongest geometric figures; pressure on one side tends to be distributed around and across it. Pressure on the pyramid can cause it to implode or explode.

• *A comprehensive approach to change*. The Collaborative Method looks at the total organization as the unit of change, with a commitment to transforming all aspects of the business: its customers, culture, work relationships, business strategy, business processes, leadership, organizational structure, and systems.

• *Behavioral change as cultural change*. The only way we really know that the organization has changed is when people's behaviors change—e.g., when the executive moves from influence management to collaborative decision making, or when someone who is abusive toward subordinates is no longer tolerated. The Collaborative Method uses the team formation process at all levels of the company to begin redefining the workplace culture in the context of designing and implementing the change effort. This creates the essential foundation for positive behavioral change.

• *A results-driven plan of action*. To build value and credibility, the Collaborative Method requires that both short- and long-term results be defined and action plans be put in place to produce them. The tools and processes are only valuable to the extent that they produce results in terms of customers, employees, and profitability.

- *Real work done in real time.* This method uses a multiple track system so that the customer and ongoing work do not suffer while the change process is moving forward. Wherever possible, the existing teams or work groups are brought together to focus on key issues while they reinvent the business.

How the Collaborative Method Works

The Collaborative Method uses a Venn diagram to represent the various elements of the work environment, all of which are addressed in this approach to change. (See Figure 7–4.) Each aspect of this figure is defined below, but it is critical to remember that the change process starts with the redefinition of the workplace culture, as evidenced by the arrow. It is also important to remember that the Venn diagram represents the interdependencies among all parts of the organization, and shows what types of interactions exist among them. The larger circle represents the external boundary of the company (external market forces and customers, for example). Inside that circle is everything that goes on within the company, such as work processes and organizational structure. Let's look at this diagram one element at a time.

- *Vision and strategic direction.* The vision defines the company's identity and its strategic direction based on its unique and value-added role and competitive advantage in the marketplace.
- *Customer relationships.* There are external and internal customers. The quality of these relationships, the way customers are treated, and their level of satisfaction are central concerns to every business.
- *Workplace culture.* The culture includes the values, principles, beliefs, customs, mores, habits, language, energy, pride, commitment, and loyalty of the workforce. The workplace culture drives an organization's productivity—which in turn is responsible for its competitive position.
- *Work processes.* There are several types of work processes, or

Figure 7–4. The Collaborative Method.

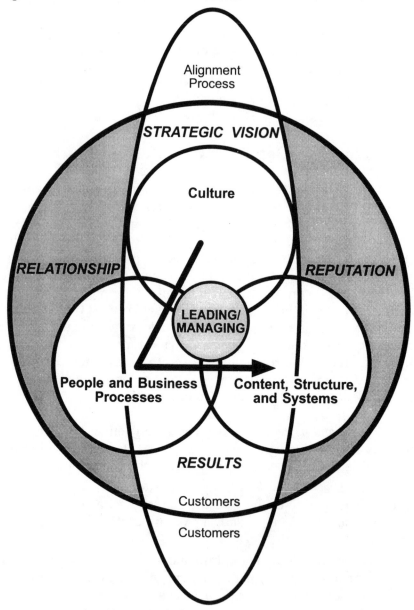

ways in which work gets done. The first type includes "people processes" that involve decision making, problem solving, planning, and conflict management. These processes may involve two or more individuals, teams, divisions, or whole departments. They may be single-function in focus, multifunctional, or even cross-functional. The second type includes business processes that ultimately deliver value to the customer, such as the supply chain that moves from procurement to manufacturing to sales and service.

▪ *Content, structures, and systems.* Content is what the company does and how it is organized. This includes its products or services, its structure as evidenced by the organization chart, and its systems groups, such as human resources, finance, administration, information systems, and legal.

▪ *Leading and managing.* At the intersection of all three inner circles we find the leadership and management functions. It is the responsibility of leaders and managers to understand not only what is in each of the organizational elements but the interactions and relationships among these elements, and to manage them for alignment, effectiveness, efficiency, and integrity.

▪ *Alignment.* In our model, the ellipse that runs from the top of the external circle through the Venn diagram and encompasses the customers represents the process of alignment, and to some extent measures the degree to which the elements of the organization are in alignment. Alignment will be one of four types:

1. *Strategic alignment* in terms of the marketplace
2. *Customer alignment* by all business and people processes, as well as the products and services delivered
3. *Workforce and cultural alignment* to ensure that the full energies and productivity of the workforce are engaged and brought to bear on the company's vision and strategic plan
4. *Leadership alignment* to ensure that leaders and members alike are in accord on the strategic direction, business and people processes, and products and services being delivered

The process of alignment involves creating a shared view or perception about what the organization is, what it ought to be doing, its direction, and how its employees will work together. Without alignment in these four key areas of action, the organization's effectiveness will suffer, workforce productivity will decline, and bottom-line results will reflect disconnects.

- *Relationships.* The character of any organization's work relationships is a function of how the values, beliefs, and mores of the workplace culture are reflected in its people and business processes. Disconnects occur when these two areas are out of alignment. For example, if there is a clear value for consensus decision making on core issues for the business and yet only a few make the decisions, there will be a basic disconnect in the work relationships of the company.

- *Results.* The quality of the company's output is a function of the alignment between its work processes and the products or services the business delivers. Disconnects occur when these two areas are out of alignment—e.g., if there is a focus on total customer service in bringing retail products to the public and yet the finance function consistently reduces the funds available for improving customer service.

- *Reputation.* Perhaps the most important credential any organization has is its reputation, which is how its values and beliefs are reflected in its products, services, and customer focus. An example of a disconnect is when a brokerage house claims to be providing the highest-quality service at the lowest cost, and then an audit discovers there is a widespread kickback scheme among the brokers.

How Do We Use the Collaborative Method?

The primary use of the Collaborative Method is to create and manage a Collaborative Workplace. In the creation process we use the method to design, implement, and realign the culture, processes, and structure of the business from hierarchy, silos, and command-and-control, to collaboration. This approach to change management is not done *to or for the company*. By its very definition, the Collaborative Method of organizational transformation is done *with and by the members* of the company.

There is a second use of the Collaborative Method as a diagnostic tool for management and teams. Through the various inventories and analyses that are conducted while the company goes through its realignment processes, critical data are generated on all aspects of the organization's operations that show where there are successes, mediocre performance, and breakdowns. Using these data, management and teams can make the appropriate interventions and improvements. If the collaborative values are already in place, there will be a high level of buy-in to this process, significantly reducing the time it takes to fix a breakdown.

The third use of the method is as a measurement tool. In effect, the diagnostic assessment at the beginning of the change process benchmarks the organization. Every 6 to 12 months these same measures may be used to determine progress toward milestones. These data can become central to a comprehensive business and organization development planning process that allocates scarce resources to the places where it will add the greatest value.

Summary

The transformation of any organization from hierarchy to collaboration is at best a difficult process. But if we have learned anything from decades of experience with "change management programs" that restructure companies, it is that they do not produce long-term competitive advantage. Hopefully, we have a greater appreciation of the power of the workplace culture and of the role it plays in driving the effectiveness of our companies. In fact, we are now coming to realize that the only way to tap into the hidden productivity, creative energy, pride, and commitment of our people is to fully and proactively engage them in the transformation process.

By using a collaborative process for engagement, we recognize the fundamental role played by basic values like respect, trust, self-esteem, and integrity in the lifeblood of the corporation. By harnessing these values to an organized set of tools and processes, the Collaborative Method provides an effective and efficient vehicle for truly transforming the organization.

8

Transforming
the Workplace

*As I grow older, I pay less attention to what men say. I just watch
what they do.*

—*Andrew Carnegie*

The new leadership at Sydex, a technology-based company, knew
that its board had very high expectations of it. Financially, the company had just been through a devastating three years. The leaders
knew they had to either reduce costs by 30 percent or increase
productivity by 25 percent to get back in the game. The company's
financial and organizational pain was great, and a major change
process was clearly needed. The leaders, however, had watched
other companies tackle similar challenges by instituting drastic
cost reductions, reengineering and downsizing, flattening the hierarchy, and stripping out thousands of jobs. The loyalty and productivity of their people had been damaged. The new leaders at Sydex
did not want to repeat those mistakes. They also did not quite
know how they were going to create this change, but they believed
that if they invested in their people, there was untapped productive energy they could engage to leapfrog the competition.

Sydex's leaders also knew that in using this investment approach to change, they would make mistakes. Even so, they decided to bet on their people. They wanted to try something that
would enable them to retain the intellectual assets, loyalty, and
productivity of their people. They decided to try an approach
based on the principle of collaboration that would engage the
workforce directly in the change process and open up the possibil-

ity of a different outcome. They had little to lose and a lot to gain. They could always slash and burn.

Where Chapter 6 focused on transforming groups of people into collaborative teams, this chapter concentrates on the processes involved in transforming an entire organization into a Collaborative Workplace. We will follow the Sydex change team as it works through the various phases of the Collaborative Method and explore the specific steps Sydex took as it created its own Collaborative Workplace.

Applying the Collaborative Method

As the Sydex team began its journey, it agreed on one very important thing: collaborative values already existed in the Sydex workforce, and all the team really had to do was to give them a chance. Even though the team did not know exactly how the process would work, it decided to challenge the workforce to take full responsibility for the success of the business. The team also knew that it would have to overcome 30 years of distrust and skepticism, and a concern that management would abandon any new program if it did not yield immediate financial results.

The Sydex leadership shared the view that the success of this change process would depend on its commitment to follow through, on its patience, and on its process skills. The leadership team realized that to transform the dominant culture from one of compliance to one of trust it would need to remember to walk the talk, engage the workforce for buy-in, build strategic alignment, establish collaborative teams, and redesign basic systems. It also knew that to succeed, it needed to believe in the Sydex people and always make decisions based on principle.

The team was aware that using the Collaborative Method to transform Sydex would mean shifting the organization's culture rather than its structure. First, it would have to get companywide alignment on the core values that would be used to lead and manage the organization as a whole. Then, since the team knew all too well that any organizational change tends to be evolutionary rather than revolutionary, it would have to create a process that gave the people at Sydex the time they needed to change their mind-sets and behaviors. If the change were done *to* or *for* them, it would not take hold; it would have to be done *by* them. Finally, the team knew that it had to work on the assumption that the workforce *wanted* to be responsible and *wanted* to do the right thing for the company.

But wasn't this just another, more sophisticated rationale for downsizing? Not at all. In choosing the Collaborative Method, the team was choosing to base the transformation on principle, not on technique, and on culture first rather than structure first. If structural change were required, the Collaborative Method would ensure some level of buy-in from the entire organization. Like the Strategic Alignment Method for focusing business strategy, the Collaborative Method invested heavily in building agreement among the leaders, members, and other key stakeholders of the organization.

At Sydex, collaborative change was not imposed, it was *engaged*. The payoff was substantial. Rather than lower productivity, the workforce at Sydex moved into overdrive because they were involved. The quality of decisions made, work produced, and service to the customer all increased dramatically. Within nine months, human productivity doubled and costs began to come down as the new work processes kicked in. Within 15 months, the financial benefits of the change began to show up on the bottom line as profits went from −2 to 5.7 percent. Year two held great promise. As the workforce gradually realized that the Collaborative Workplace was not just another structural program but the new way they would do business, commitment to the new culture became irreversible.

The Collaborative Method used by Sydex has five phases, with a number of steps within each phase. These phases (represented in Figure 8–1) are: need and commitment; preparing for the change; assessment, alignment, and plan; managing implementation; and self-sufficiency and renewal.

Phase 1: Need and Commitment

No change process can be successful unless it is absolutely clear that the change is critically needed to ensure organizational success and that there is a specific methodology for implementing it.

Figure 8–1. The five phases of the Collaborative Method.

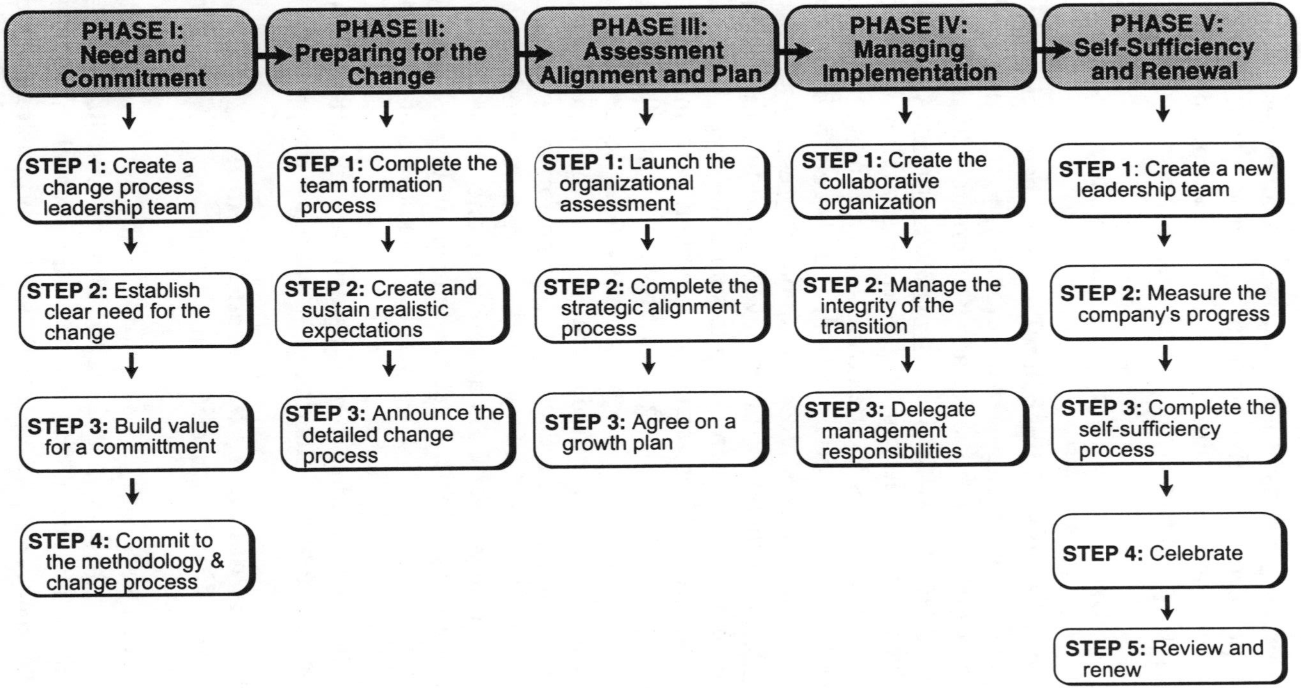

PHASE I: Need and Commitment
- STEP 1: Create a change process leadership team
- STEP 2: Establish clear need for the change
- STEP 3: Build value for a commitment
- STEP 4: Commit to the methodology & change process

PHASE II: Preparing for the Change
- STEP 1: Complete the team formation process
- STEP 2: Create and sustain realistic expectations
- STEP 3: Announce the detailed change process

PHASE III: Assessment Alignment and Plan
- STEP 1: Launch the organizational assessment
- STEP 2: Complete the strategic alignment process
- STEP 3: Agree on a growth plan

PHASE IV: Managing Implementation
- STEP 1: Create the collaborative organization
- STEP 2: Manage the integrity of the transition
- STEP 3: Delegate management responsibilities

PHASE V: Self-Sufficiency and Renewal
- STEP 1: Create a new leadership team
- STEP 2: Measure the company's progress
- STEP 3: Complete the self-sufficiency process
- STEP 4: Celebrate
- STEP 5: Review and renew

The purpose of Phase 1 is to ensure basic alignment at all levels of the organization on the need to change and win a fundamental and irrevocable commitment to move forward. The Collaborative Method used at Sydex was a four-step process.

Step 1: Creating a Change Process Leadership Team

Someone has to start the ball rolling and then stick with the process all the way through. An effective way to build long-term value for the Collaborative Workplace is to create a leadership team of key members who will drive the change process. Great care must be given to their selection and recruitment. They must be people who: (1) will model the behavior; (2) have the requisite skills; (3) are respected by the organization; and (4) believe in the change. It is best if the team is cross-functional, represents all parts of the company, and involves several levels, including the top manager. The team needs to be freed up to spend the time. This is a significant commitment for each team member, with meetings and responsibilities often taking an average of 20 to 30 percent of the team members' time. There will also need to be an agreement about how their other obligations will be fulfilled and how their participation will be reflected in their performance reviews.

At Sydex, the CEO formed and participated on a seven-member change team. As anticipated, one of the first questions people asked during the initial engagement process was: "Is Steve (the CEO) involved?" They wanted to know that top leadership was directly engaged.

The team decided to hold its first meeting off-site. The objective was to determine its degree of value for the process.

Step 2: Establishing the Need to Change the Work Environment

Sydex had just changed its executive team. Financial results, as we saw earlier, had been quite poor and showed little hope of improvement in spite of drastic cost cutting over the past three years. The company was losing market share, and customers were publicly voicing their unhappiness. The workforce felt devalued and was anxious about the next round of layoffs. Morale was at an all-time low. Simply reorganizing the company again would not solve its problems.

For any significant transformation process to work there must first be a *burning platform*—a clear recognition by key stakeholders that "insanity" is continuing to do the same things while expecting different results. There must be a realization that the costs of not changing are greater than the costs of changing, and that changing the structure is an insufficient response.

At the same time, there may be considerable *denial* about the need to change. If profits are up or going up, the refrain is, "If it ain't broke, don't fix it." If profits are down or going down, the view is likely to be, "We don't have the money to invest right now; we have to cut costs." There may also be a strongly held view that structural change will fix everything. In other words, in the world of denial, there is no good time to change the way the company has been doing things. Denial most often occurs when people feel threatened by major change. They may fear losing their base of power or control. They may not want to be accountable to others. It is very uncomfortable to change. Their egos are involved. Or their last experience with a change program was so painful that they do not want to go through it again.

It may not be popular to be willing to move beyond denial, to identify the need for change and take a stand for doing something new. At Sydex, there was a fairly high level of denial among three members of senior management. They wanted to see the reengineering process finished before any new change was introduced. They also believed that the new incentive system would shift behavior. Other team members, however, felt that it was time to shift the culture of the workplace and create a work environment where people truly felt valued. The company's downsizing had cut into the meat of the organization, and their credibility was suffering. It was time to try a different tack.

There is usually some *precipitating event* that causes the change process to begin. At Sydex it was poor financial performance and the changing of the executive team. At other companies it may be the loss of a major customer, a labor strike, a merger/acquisition, or an executive who has had a life-changing experience and wants to leave a legacy of hope, growth, and positive change. But although events like these may precipitate an awareness of the need to change, they do not necessarily guarantee the *willingness to change*. The distinction here is between an intellectual understanding of a situation and the behavioral shift required to commit resources to effect its resolution. The Sydex team was willing to explore new ways of working together, to learn about collaborative principles and processes.

Step 3: Building Value for a Commitment

Any change process is most vulnerable to termination in its early stages, especially before an executive commitment has been made. At Sydex, the team learned that a verbal or intellectual commitment to change was very different from the commitment of actual time, talents, and finances to make it a reality. Reality set in when the team members got out their calendars to schedule the first three months of meetings.

From the very beginning, the Sydex team realized that the collaborative change process would require *continuous value building* across the organization and among key stakeholders. Moreover, it realized that it must emphasize the expected *benefits and results*, not the process itself. The change process was merely a vehicle, a means to an end. The team also learned that it could not build value by focusing on the abstract idea of cultural change. Whatever the activity, the Sydex team had to consistently position the change effort in concrete business terms, with the collaborative process being applied to such real business issues as setting a new strategic direction, enhancing customer relationships, and building a collaborative strategic alliance with a major business partner.

The Sydex team wasted no time about going directly to *key stakeholders*—members of the board, important customers, and top leadership in the company—to engage them in an early assessment of the current state of Sydex. The objective was to validate whether there was indeed a burning platform and to build value for the need to transform the organization. The team members found that the board's executive committee was already dissatisfied with many aspects of the organization's performance and was quite willing to consider a different approach to change. The team got the board's tacit support up-front.

There are usually several influential members of the organization who have serious objections to the change process. *Influential resisters* need to be engaged early on to determine the level of their disagreement. In one midsize services company, there was a senior vice president who, when she did not agree with a direction being taken, would stand in the hall and talk to everyone coming by and tell them how terrible it was that this action was being taken. Within hours, the entire organization would be buzzing about her viewpoint. More often than not, the process was either aborted or substantially changed. No one was willing to confront her. Resistant behavior of this kind needs to be addressed directly and quickly.

One of the three people who had major objections to the proposed change at Sydex was unwilling even to talk about the change. The team had agreed on the basic principle that no one person should be allowed to dictate the direction of the company. To this end it used two tools: root-cause analysis and an engagement strategy called "increase the stakes," which involved the entire organization in building value for the process throughout the workforce. Within two months, the team had gotten the holdout's buy-in.

In the early weeks of the Sydex change process, there were varying degrees of *workforce commitment* to the effort. About 10 percent of the workforce were what can be called heat seekers, people eager to make a dramatic shift in their work environment and refocus on the customer. Another 10 to 15 percent were dead set against it; they thought things were just fine and more change was unnecessary. The balance of the workforce were "from Missouri"; they were willing to believe the process would work, but wanted the change team to *show* them it would work. The Sydex team was able to get the latter group to buy in at a basic level so that things could move forward. Meantime, there was a grace period of about 90 days before some concrete changes were needed.

Step 4: Committing to the Methodology

It was not long before people began asking what would happen next. The members of the change team were able to fend off the

Figure 8–2. The Collaborative Arrow.

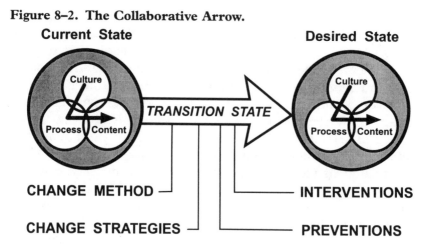

pressure for a precise answer for a month, but during that month the team knew it had to adopt a methodology and a specific set of steps and processes that could be presented to the organization. It also knew it would be using the Collaborative Method, and had in fact already committed to the *methodology* in principle. Now it needed to get into the specifics.

The Sydex team began the process with a tool called the Collaborative Arrow, which enabled the group to think about the change process from a comprehensive perspective. (See Figure 8–2.) Using this tool, the Sydex team was able to simultaneously: (1) consider all elements of the organization that would be changed; (2) establish a basis for measuring change over time; and (3) consider proactively the specific method, strategies, preventions, and interventions that would be made to ensure success.

As the team members worked through the *current-state analysis*, they soon realized the complexity of what they were trying to do. It was a multifaceted challenge and involved dealing with a wide range of issues all at once. The current culture was one of skepticism, anger, and compliance. They knew they were not getting the best from the workforce and that recent structural changes had exacerbated their dilemma.

The team members invested some time in creating their *desired state vision* for the organization as well as their desired business objectives. The more involved Strategic Alignment Method would be applied later. The idea here was to identify where they wanted Sydex to go as a business. Its desired state was not as easy as they had thought it would be to articulate. The various members had significant differences about what type of company they wanted it to become. At this point they realized the real value of engaging the organization: It had to be everyone's vision for the future.

The team then specifically mapped out its desired outcomes for the change process and outlined the *transition state,* or specific strategies: It would use to get there.

The Collaborative Method calls for lots of interaction, discussion, and agreement as the process proceeds. One of the worst things that can happen in a change process is that the change team gets too far out in front, only to look around and find no one behind it.

Another thing that can happen is that the team does not fully appreciate its *limitations.* People are usually quite enthusiastic when the change process starts off. They are hopeful and expect miracles. There is a tendency to wax eloquent about what will be accomplished without truly understanding the limitations of the group, the land mines in the path ahead, and the unforeseen circumstances that can derail the effort. With a healthy respect for these limitations, the process can be less frustrating.

It is even more important that the group be sure it has *a commitment to proceed.* Just because people say they agree does not mean they do. Some people will silently disagree while verbally agreeing because they know that disagreeing with a key corporate direction can result in serious career consequences. In the movement toward a Collaborative Workplace, however, special attention must be given to this phenomenon. Its existence should be recognized, and a different way to register disagreement should be made available. The environment must be free from fear or reprisals. The attitude and tone of top leadership will help shift the pendulum toward more open exchange.

At the level where resources must be committed, the agreement to proceed must be explicit, clear, and irrevocable. Once the expected results for the change have been defined and the methodology clarified, the commitment to proceed means no turning back. There may be fine-tuning, realignment, or adjustments to the strategy along the way, but if there is lurking in the background any idea of a trapdoor or escape hatch that can be used to bail out of the process, the integrity of the process will be at risk.

Phase 2: Preparing for the Change

The change team at Sydex knew that even with agreement to move forward, it needed to continue building value. In completing its preparations for the full transformation, it used a three-step process.

Step 1: Completing the Team Formation Process

It was now time for the Sydex change team to begin creating the Collaborative Workplace by modeling the process themselves. The team worked through the collaborative team formation process (see Chapter 6), starting with task definition and the creation of Operating Agreements. Like many teams before them, they came face-to-face with two key issues: a sense of urgency and building trust.

The task of designing and implementing the transformation of an organization involves a great *sense of urgency*. There is often a reluctance to do a lot of process work. But you either *invest up front or pay later*, and keep on paying for poor-quality decisions. For example, without its consensus-based Operating Agreements, a team's initial conflicts or disagreements will take much longer to resolve or may not get resolved at all. As disagreements accumulate or confidences are breached, the integrity and trust in the team will drop and team spirit and effectiveness will dissipate. It is far more cost-effective and efficient to take the time up-front and put the prevention in place.

In its Operating Agreements process, the change team at Sydex found it had two areas of fundamental disagreement: confidentiality and consensus. Much time was spent getting to the root cause of these issues, and they were successfully resolved. This was a new experience for many members of the team. In the past they had always hidden their differences or talked about them behind the others' backs. Now it was as if the floodgates had opened.

They were finally talking about the things that really mattered to them, the things that would truly make a difference in how they worked together. *Trust and confidence* went up. They now knew that breakthroughs in their own relationships were possible, and, as a result, believed they could succeed and be good role models.

Step 2: Creating and Sustaining Realistic Expectations

One definition of an upset is that it is an unfulfilled expectation. At Sydex the expectations of the workforce soared as soon as the team announced the company's intention to change the work environment. But every member had a different set of expectations. Some wanted to be empowered and left alone. Others wanted more direct accountability. Still others were hopeful that finally they would get to use their talents in a more productive way. Clearly, there was no alignment of expectations; in fact, for several weeks they were allowed to run rampant, creating an informal wish list for change that would probably not withstand the test of time. When the change team found out about these widely varying expectations, it committed itself to establishing a more realistic framework immediately.

There is perhaps nothing more critical in Phase 2 than setting *realistic expectations* for the change process. The lower the expectations, the better. One rule of thumb is to downplay the probable outcomes and let the workforce be pleasantly surprised. The trick for any change team is how to sell the benefits of the process without overselling the outcomes.

One way to establish more realistic expectations is to provide the workforce with a clear understanding about *the ups and downs of change*. They need to know where the pitfalls are and what the critical success factors will be. Figure 8–3 is helpful in showing how a successful change process looks over time. There are always ups and downs in the process. What we want to see is an upward trend over time. To ensure this trend, it is critical that leadership anticipate when process interventions are needed and be ready to implement them.

A central issue at this stage of the process is to reach *critical mass*, which occurs when the collaborative culture has taken hold sufficiently for the process to sustain itself. Even though critical

Figure 8–3. The psychology of the change process.

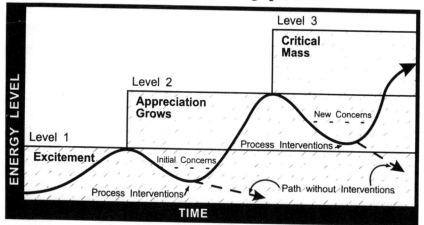

mass usually occurs well into the implementation phase, the team must stay vigilant to ensure that hopes and dreams remain consistent with reality. Critical mass may not happen easily. As Figure 8–3 demonstrates, there is more than one point in the process at which interventions may be needed to manage the effort toward success.

One problem the Sydex team ran into early on was the vehemence with which the proposed process was attacked by skeptics. The "bulls" among them tried outright assaults on the credibility of the process by calling its methods into question, while others challenged the team composition and used sarcasm to trivialize the objectives of the process. The "submarines" manipulated the informal networks to make clear that they had no belief in the effort. Meanwhile, the "elephants" indicated that if the process failed, they would not forget and would be there to remind everyone that it had not worked.

Threats like these to the integrity of the start-up process must be handled as soon as they show up. The up-front and early engagement of all members and stakeholders of the organization will go a long way toward mitigating these problems. A key to success is not allowing a vacuum to emerge in which a few vocal skeptics can operate unchallenged. Unfortunately, even though we are working to install a collaborative culture, we are often doing so in an unwelcome, or at least *a skeptical, environment*. Sometimes we must match the existing culture and challenge it to operate by the new rules. We must be very careful to model the way.

As the saying goes, "nothing succeeds like success." This is especially true in a transformation process. To build value and momentum for change, it is wise to bring about some *early visible successes*, things that have needed doing for some time or things that will demonstrate to the organization that there is truly a new culture beginning to take hold.

At one company that began this process in earnest, the staff felt that management really needed to find a way to work together as a team. As part of its early visible successes, the change team identified three short-term projects that all of them could participate in jointly. The leaders were seen in public working together. With time, it became clear to even the most skeptical that top-level collaboration was possible.

The change team at Sydex did the same thing. It set several practical business targets to highlight its work and focus the attention of the workforce. One target was securing a new contract with a major customer the company had been seeking for several years. Another target was producing a new software application that Sydex's current customers wanted in half the usual time. Yet another target was developing the new covenant. As each of these major milestones was met, the leadership team held a major celebration for the entire organization and acknowledged the teams and individuals responsible for the success.

Step 3: *Announcing the Detailed Change Process*

The Sydex team did not sit on its hands during Phase 2. It worked out all the details, methods, and tools that would be used to move into Phase 3, when the assessment and alignment processes were scheduled to begin. The measures to be used in the organizational assessment were agreed to, the road map was nailed down, roles and responsibilities were assigned, the budget was adopted, and the probable land mines were anticipated. The team was ready to roll.

Phase 3: Assessment, Alignment, and Plan

It would have made little sense for the Sydex team to begin its journey without knowing its starting point or what would indicate that it had reached its goals. The current-state assessment had given the team a high-level picture of where it was, but it needed a more complete assessment—one that provided both quantitative and qualitative benchmarks for the entire organization. At the same time, the group knew it needed to align the organization and build value for a new strategic direction. (See Chapter 5.) The result was a growth plan that looked specifically at how Sydex would achieve its expected results. This was a three-step process.

Step 1: Launching the Organizational Assessment

Sydex's organizational assessment needed to be as comprehensive as possible. It was designed to establish an objective starting point; some of the information was difficult to hear, but it was also necessary to know. The assessment made it possible to draw distinctions between perception and fact and provided a platform for converting complaints into positive, responsible actions. The three primary arenas in which the team began to collect data were: the business and the customer; workplace relationships and processes; and organization systems. A wide array of measurement tools was used. It was particularly important to get some quantitative read on the well-being of the workplace culture.

Based on its rather exhaustive assessment, the Sydex team was able to determine series of benchmark starting points for the change process. It also used this information to determine the most appropriate and effective types of change interventions.

The Sydex team believed that by continuing to engage the membership of the organization to help in the assessment, it could continue to build value for what needed to change. The group engaged a committee representative of the board as well as several cross-functional groups in the organization. It also asked Sydex's key customers to participate, a move that overlapped with the Strategic Alignment Method as discussed in Chapter 5.

We don't just wake up one day and realize that the way we have been doing things at companies is all wrong. We have done them that way for a reason that once seemed to make sense. But now we have to open our minds to new ways of thinking about what we have been doing and how well. By nature, this is an *iterative process*. People have to have time to gradually hear that what they have been doing is less effective than it needs to be. Some may think that shocking the system works—it doesn't. Shocking the organization only causes people to dig in and cling to their positions. They need to be engaged, facilitated, educated, incented, and coaxed out of their paradigms about how best to run the business.

During Phase 2 at Sydex, some people began to ask questions about when the "real work" was going to get done. To address this very practical concern, work went forward on *several tracks* simultaneously:

Track 1:   Completing the business at hand
Track 2:   Completing the various phases of the change
            process
Track 3:   Building internal skills for self-sufficiency

Steps 2 and 3: Strategic Alignment and Growth Plan

The next two steps have been discussed in detail in Chapter 5. It is essential, however, that throughout this process several considerations be kept in mind. First, the change team needs to remain objective, facilitative, and dedicated to operating on principle. There will be competition for influence over the company's direction and even questions about who should really be making this or that decision. The team must remain firm in its resolve and work to ensure the integrity of the process.

Second, the team must watch for hidden agendas, nonalignment, and less-than-full participation. Often things may not be what they seem. A false alignment at this stage can be dangerous later on. The team must ferret out the different needs of key players and get them on the table. It is vital to actively engage those who are quiet or who are withholding their perspectives. *Full and open engagement* is essential.

Third, the team must treat all customers like family. In addition to a more formal full-value contracting process, the team should make sure that the customers' perspective has been fully heard and that alignment results are reviewed with them prior to release. It is equally important that the change team ensure that the key stakeholders are in agreement with the new direction.

Phase 4: Managing Implementation

As the CEO looked out at the 15 Sydex board members, he realized how far they had come as a team. It was just six months ago that the change team had asked the board's approval for resources to support this planning process. At that time the board did not particularly care whether the company was run by command-and-control or collaborative teams. It was chiefly interested in financial results. As a result of the strategic alignment and organizational assessment processes, however, the questions asked at this meeting were quite different. The chairman was asking about the real level of buy-in among the staff. He wanted to know if the company would be able to avoid laying off people by increasing productivity. He even asked a question about how the teams would now be able to make Sydex more competitive.

The CEO knew they were ready to embark on the implementation phase of this journey. The change team had a true consensus agreement on the growth plan, the staff had reached a 75 percent level of buy-in, and the customers were quite happy that they had become the central focus of Sydex's new direction. Now the change team faced a whole new set of issues. The three steps in this phase of its work seemed relatively simple, but in reality would take a considerable amount of care and feeding. (Note: It is important that these steps be considered in conjunction with Chapter 9, which discusses what it takes to ensure the integrity of the transition process.)

Step 1: Creating the Collaborative Workplace

The collaborative team formation and management process have already been discussed. But what about the dynamics of the change process that the *organization* will encounter as it tries to put this approach into practice?

The Sydex change team had prepared a document for distribution that spelled out the growth plan, its expected results, the specific strategies to be employed, the new structure, and the roles and responsibilities of the various teams in the implementation process. The team members had also made a pact among themselves that this was going to be a quality change process, that they would *do it right*. The pressures to implement before they were ready were severe. But they knew how important it was to have full ownership and agreement on the plan. At least one member of the team pointed out that these pressures were really a positive sign and that they should not interpret them as a desire by the organization to put the new culture in place. The team held the line, and later was glad that it had.

It is not easy to make the transition from command-and-control to collaboration. The last thing the change team wanted to do was to send the organization into shock. Therefore, the plan called for the bifurcation of member reporting relationships in *an administrative/functional split* that would help ease the transition and keep the workforce focused while the culture change began to take effect. Each workforce member was assigned to one team as a home base in accordance with his or her functional expertise. Each team would go through the collaborative team formation process and agree on the roles of the leadership function.

Each employee would also have an administrative reporting relationship. The reporting, however, would not necessarily be to the person designated as interim "team leader." For 50 percent of their performance evaluation, members would report to a team sponsor, who might have a span of control as high as 1:50. The other half of the evaluation would come from the individual's team. As the organization evolved, these percentages might change; the performance review process would certainly change.

The plan called for the development of internal *self-sufficiency* in managing the change process. As the change team anticipated the rollout to the organization, it initiated a skills-development process that would eventually equip 25 percent of its members with the requisite skills to help lead and manage the change process. The initial round was focused on those individuals who would begin forming teams to launch the effort.

Timing is everything in the change business. It was critical that the change team involve the workforce at precisely the right moment. The Sydex team decided to engage the entire organization in groups of 20 over a period of two months in the first round of skills development. These workshops focused on what it meant to be a full member of a Collaborative Workplace. The intention of this *just-in-time engagement* was not training per se, but preparing members for active participation in the teams they had been assigned to. It was a level set, and was designed to lay to rest any remaining doubts about senior management's commitment to putting this new cultural foundation in place.

It worked. Nearly all the members participated, and fewer than 1 percent left with any serious negative perspectives on the process. Clearly all the preparation work and initial engagement efforts had paid off. There were no surprises, only eagerness to move toward critical mass.

Step 2: *Managing the Integrity of the Transition*

Integrity is defined by Webster as "soundness, honesty, firm adherence to a code of moral values." As we will see in Chapter 9, there are many opportunities in the change process for disconnects, or breaches in integrity, as a company becomes a Collaborative Workplace. Our focus here is to explore how several of those disconnects affected the Sydex transition, and how its change team responded.

Six months into the transition, the Sydex board decided to merge two of the company's seven departments to better position the company for an anticipated acquisition. The decision caught most of the change team members by surprise. The CEO had known but had kept the move quiet as part of his agreement with the board. At an emergency meeting, an outside mediator was engaged to process a range of serious questions the team had about the CEO's credibility and accountability for the success of the team and the change process. Two members even threatened to resign.

After hours of debate, however, the team came to a better understanding about why the deal had been kept secret, the conflict the CEO had felt, and how it would move forward with both the change effort and the acquisition. New commitments were made to put all the business as well as the change issues on the table for full discussion. The team's Operating Agreements were amended to reflect this event, and at a joint meeting with the board, a set of agreements was created that established how the two groups would work together.

No team will be able to anticipate everything that may happen, but it must remain vigilant and *expect the unexpected*. It must take nothing for granted. And when the worst-case scenario happens, as it did at Sydex, it must be prepared to revisit its resolve and stick to its principles, even in the face of what may feel like insurmountable obstacles.

It was not long after the functional teams at Sydex were formed that the change team began to notice another phenomenon—team members began to behave as if their teams were the new turf, the new silos. Loyalty was to the team rather than to the company. They began to hear, "I cannot help you because my team . . ." Loyalty to the primary teams had become very strong if for no other reason than that the collaborative team formation process had brought them together so effectively. It was all too easy for team members to make the team the new silo and focus their energy on protecting it. Old behaviors die hard.

The Sydex team recognized that, while the strategic leadership team was clear about where *its* loyalties lay, the rest of the membership had become conflicted. It decided to engage everyone in an off-site discussion about this issue, invoke the collaborative problem-solving process, and create a team code of conduct about the responsibilities of each team to the company as a whole. Specific behaviors were identified, and a process for future problem resolution was agreed to. When the retreat was over, it was clear to the change team that shifting loyalty from the work group to the company as a whole was a fundamental step in the journey to the new culture.

Step 3: Delegating Management Responsibilities

By the end of the first year, the collaborative process had moved into full swing as teams took on their functional responsibilities with some ease. The boundary issues between teams had been worked out and their integrity issues resolved. The Sydex change team felt it was ready to begin the next part of the implementation process: the *delegation of routine management responsibilities* to the teams. It was clear that no one knew better what their specific personnel and budgetary requirements were than the teams themselves. Similarly, the board began to see the teams as a critical resource in planning the growth of the business for the next year. At one meeting, two members of the change team suddenly came to the same realization: If they delegated these responsibilities to the teams, they themselves would be freed up to focus on key strategic issues.

Here was a major payoff for having moved to a Collaborative Workplace. Because the change team now had a high degree of trust and confidence in the alignment and accountability of the teams, there was no longer a need to control or manage them. Instead, it could give them more to do. With a careful analysis of all the functions that management had retained in the old way of working, it identified fully 75 percent that could now be delegated to the teams at a rate commensurate with their capacity and readiness. The teams were excited, and the transfer went off without a hitch. Sydex had reached critical mass and was on its way to self-sufficiency.

Phase 5: Self-Sufficiency and Renewal

Like most aspects of this process, the idea of self-sufficiency means different things to different people. To some it may mean that they can handle any change issue that comes their way. To others it may mean that they have developed a whole new level of process skill and confidence. To still others it may mean that there is no more need for a change team to guide them through the process. Self-sufficiency may even mean that leadership knows enough about the process to know when to ask for help.

There really is no one right answer. It evolves based on each organization's needs and experiences. But because the Collaborative Workplace is not a project or a program but a way of life, self-sufficiency does mean that the organization has developed a fairly high level of internal capacity to manage the continued development, learning, and maturation of that workplace. It means it knows how to manage the integrity of the transition, how to integrate what it has learned about itself into a growth process, and when to begin the process of renewal.

To be able to renew itself, the self-sufficient organization must be prepared to give up the structures and processes it has developed over a period of two to three years and start over again with a blank sheet. Ultimately, organizational self-sufficiency means maturity and the recognition that nothing is constant except principles and core values.

As Sydex reached this phase of the company's transformation, it entered a five-step process.

Step 1: Creating a New Leadership Team

Rotating leadership is essential if a company is to maintain a level of objectivity in this process. People get stuck over time, begin to believe their assumptions about what works best, and get emotionally and psychologically invested in holding on to what they have created. Rotation must be a clear, up-front expectation for all members of the team. It not only reflects a commitment to the psychological health of the organization, but opens up a career development opportunity for members who have excelled as situational leaders.

Step 2: Measuring the Company's Progress

During the assessment phase, the change team had developed a comprehensive set of *measures* to benchmark the organization. Now that it was more than a year down the road, it was time to measure progress. This time, however, every team in the company was given significant responsibility for generating and analyzing the data. The Workplace Culture Index was used again to assess progress toward a collaborative work environment. Each of the teams got back its results, and decisions were made about what changes were needed.

Step 3: Completing Self-Sufficiency Skills Development

It was now time for Sydex to complete its initial cycle of change. The change team had identified about 20 percent of the workforce that it wanted to develop as a cadre of *skilled change agents*. The change team provided them with an additional four weeks of intensive certification training. They could now manage Sydex through the next round of business planning and organizational change. These individuals also went through a level of self-study and completed their personal journeys.

In effect, Sydex had created its own internal consulting organization. They coached one another, providing moral and professional support for themselves and others. By institutionalizing this capability, Sydex was now truly self-sufficient.

Step 4: Celebrating Successes

The primary unit for celebration in a Collaborative Workplace is the team. At Sydex, the tradition of celebrating a team success became going out to dinner. The members of one team took their spouses on a weekend of golfing. Other teams went to athletic events or to the beach for picnics.

Perhaps the most difficult form of celebration the teams learned how to do was that of *acknowledgement*, verbally recognizing the contributions that each member had made to the success of the enterprise. The teams committed to learning how to do this because they knew how important it was to validate the worth of another person. It was an authentic appreciation of the skills, capabilities, and contributions each individual gave to the team effort. They learned that the acknowledgements process would get easier with practice and that it was very helpful in enhancing the team's level of trust.

Step 5: Reviewing and Renewing

Nothing is forever. One of the greatest dangers any organization faces is becoming static, self-satisfied, and arrogant, particularly when it is successful. How many companies have we seen in the last ten years slip off the competitive screen because they forgot to adapt to new market conditions? To combat this malaise, we must first review where and who we are. Then we have to renew.

Using the results of the measurement process, the new Sydex leadership team and a range of members from across the organization completed an *exhaustive review* of major business processes, the roles and responsibilities of teams, their customers' new requirements, and the organizational structure and systems. They asked themselves: Are they still appropriate for where they are now? Should they be eliminated? What new directions should they take? Are they still aligned, and if so, how well? What lessons had they learned from their journey so far? What could they do differently to increase their effectiveness and efficiency?

Renewal must become a regular event, undertaken at least once every few years. Each time one must start over from scratch. There are no sacred cows. The Operating Agreements must be revisited. As in the beginning of this process, a new change team once again engages the organization in the process.

Summary

As I watch my two sons grow up into young men, I am reminded of some fundamental precepts of early childhood development and how they certainly must apply to organizations. We can keep our children behaving like children by not letting them grow up, by suppressing their innate curiosity, their need to say "no" to establish their identity, and their desire to learn. We can certainly control their environment to make sure that they never get hurt. But the net effect is that they will never really develop their own sense of themselves and the ability to handle the curve balls that life will throw at them.

The process of transforming a command-and-control environment into a Collaborative Workplace is similar. We are giving birth to a new being that will have an identity of its own. It will have to say "no" at various points in order to establish its willingness to say "yes." It will make many mistakes as it tries to discover who and what it really is. And as it learns how to take care of itself, to be self-sufficient, it will be a voracious learner of new skills.

The challenge today's leadership faces is to allow organizations to make the journey, to grow up, to discover their new selves. We can be their guides and provide nurturing, a moral and ethical foundation, and a safe place to call home. We can set boundaries so they won't get hurt. We can provide an environment in which they can question, learn, and grow. We certainly want to encourage them to respect themselves and others, to have integrity and be honorable in all endeavors, to be trustworthy, take full responsibility for their own success, serve others, and be accountable for their behaviors and actions.

In this way, we are able to heal the past by creating the foundation for the future.

9

Managing the Transition

All life is an experiment. The more experiments you make, the better.
—Ralph Waldo Emerson

To realize the full value of creating a Collaborative Workplace, we must remember that collaboration is a way of life. Collaboration is a principle for transforming an organization in a way that shifts not only its foundation but also its approach to strategy, customers, its people, work processes, and systems.

To ensure the integrity of the transition to a fully operational Collaborative Workplace, every aspect of the organization must work in a way that is congruent with the new value system. If, for example, the compensation system still rewards individual behavior when everyone is working in teams, there will be a disconnect, or break, in the integrity of the organization's direction and operations with implications for the performance of the business. In the transition process to the new work culture, it is imperative that these disconnects be minimized to ensure success and long-term value.

This chapter focuses on what needs to be done to manage the transition process in such a way that disconnects are minimized and integrity is preserved. This chapter considers a range of specific implementation issues that can arise in managing the transition and explores the types of interventions that change-process managers can use in each of four areas: the leadership mind-set; business and customer; workforce relationships and processes; and organizational systems.

Building Organizational Integrity for Long-Term Value

Creating a Collaborative Workplace is like a courtship. The management of the transition process, however, is like working at a marriage—it has permanence and it takes a lot of work. Taking it for granted or breaching the integrity of the relationship can result in divorce or serious dysfunction. As we begin to manage this new organization through the early years of transitioning to a new work culture, we must carefully examine each aspect of its operations and ensure that they square with the core values of collaboration. The real payoff for going through the transformation process will be found in the efficiencies that result when the entire organization is aligned with the new value system.

Prospecting for Disconnects

Tandol Corporation's marketing literature made significant commitments to its prospective customers. Tandol would far exceed other companies as a valued business partner by assigning a team of experts to each new customer from the date of first order. In reality, this never happened. Only one person was dedicated to each customer, and most customers had to call several times to get their products serviced. The net result was that both Tandol's customer satisfaction ratings and its reputation in the market were abysmal.

A disconnect takes place when there is a significant or noticeable gap between what a company says it does or will do and what it actually does. Figure 9–1 shows that there are at least four major areas where disconnects can and do occur:

1. *Leadership.* When leaders do not walk the talk, are out of touch with the workforce, or quit the process in midstream.
2. *Business and customers.* When a business forgets its customers, focuses on short-term results, or resorts to hierarchical solutions. Evidence of disconnects in this area includes lower profits, higher dissatisfaction among customers, and negative reputation ratings.

Figure 9–1. Managing disconnects for integrity.

FOCUS	TRANSITION ISSUES	INTERVENTIONS
LEADERSHIP	Walking the Talk	• Operating Agreements • Third-party coaching • Get new leadership
	Exhibiting New Behavior	• Operating Agreements • Third-party coaching • Team coaching • 360° feedback
	Committing to Success	• Individual choice • Commitment to succeed — a choice
BUSINESS AND CUSTOMER	Remembering the Customer	• Instill customer mind-set (banners, notices, reminders) • Measurement system • Customer "Hit Squad" • Full-value contracting • Realistic expectations
	Frustration With Slow Buy-In	• Dual-track operations • Visible successes • Put the hierarchy to rest • Road map for change • Chart progress
	What Do We Do With the Hierarchy?	• Everyone on a team • Basic skills training • Redesign appraisal/compensation system • Measure effectiveness • Celebrate milestones
WORKFORCE RELATION-SHIPS AND PROCESSES	"I'm from Missouri" Doing real work Building tolerance for ambiguity Developing new skills	• Senior management walks the talk • Define the new covenant • Redefine the work culture • Real work in real time by real teams • Create collaborative teams • Operating Agreements • Establish milestones • Implement new roles and responsibilities • Identify skills needed • Provide collaborative skills training
ORGANIZATION SYSTEMS	Becoming Focused on the Internal Customer	• Customer engagement process • Meet the immediate customers' needs • Full-value contracts
	Moving From Control to Contribution	• Mind-set and behavioral change • New work processes • Evaluate and realign systems
	Realigning Organization Systems	• No sacred cows • Open up discussion • Realign all systems
	Creating a healing culture	• Cross-functional team assessment • Values review • Delegate management responsibilities to teams • 360° feedback • Results-based performance • Integrated skills-development process • Customer-driven information systems • Simplify project management systems • Make all systems user-friendly and accessible

3. *Workforce relationships and processes.* When the workforce is so alienated by the program-of-the-month approach to change and so insecure about their jobs that they resent and resist any change. Evidence of disconnects in this area includes lower productivity, higher levels of stress and absenteeism, and increased costs due to overlapping business processes.
4. *Organizational systems.* When our internal support systems are out of sync with our core values, resulting in battles for control, duplication, overlap, and inefficiency.

The Leadership Mind-Set in Transition

The executive committee at Tandol was well known for its command-and-control approach to life. Even though Tandol had invested heavily in new leadership technologies—most recently in a collaborative prototype—there was still a strong need for central control. The executives expected short-term financial results from this latest process, but after a year, they were quite prepared to recommend to the board at their next meeting that they go back to the old way of doing things. After all, it produced results and did not cost much.

The Tandol situation is not at all uncommon. In many companies, the pressure to try the new management approaches is driven by the belief that something different must be done if we are to be competitive in the 21st century. At the same time, the collaborative process is asking leadership to take a significant leap of faith and give up tried-and-true methods for managing people and businesses for competitive advantage. Why should they? What's more, when the new processes do not produce immediate bottom-line results, what should they do?

The greatest transition issues these leaders face as we move to a more collaborative approach to business are the need to: walk the talk of the new values; exhibit new behavior; and commit to success. All these issues speak to the need for a better appreciation of what they will individually have to do if there is to be integrity in the transition.

Walking the Talk

Nothing speaks louder than actions. When a senior executive of a service company regularly permitted his general counsel to go up and down the halls berating his colleagues, the commitment to collaborative behaviors was questioned. To regain integrity in this circumstance requires several related actions. The most effective prevention is the Operating Agreements process, since mutual respect and accountability are central to its effective implementation. If that does not work, there may be a need for third-party coaching to give feedback and deal with the executive's reluctance to confront the behavior. If the resistance is even more profound, there may a need to determine if it is possible for this person to manage the transition process for integrity. Usually, at this level of consultation, realignment occurs. If it does not, it may be best to wait until there is new leadership.

Exhibiting New Behavior

"Well, I tried to be open to feedback—but then George said something I felt was really wrong. Who does he think he is? He's only a director. Doesn't he know who signs his paycheck?" This is one type of reaction to change processes that focus on superficial behavioral change rather than fundamental cultural realignment. This person did take the time to go to the workshops and the weekend retreats. He "got religion" for a month, then allowed the pressures of the business to overwhelm him again.

Reversion to old behavior is one of the more serious threats to the integrity of any company's effort to become a Collaborative Workplace. It is much easier to blame the process or the program than to be willing to explore the impacts of one's own behavior and consider changing it. There are a number of interventions that can be used to produce some level of integrity, including the Operating Agreements process or third-party coaching from someone outside the management group or the organization. Team coaching can also be helpful by providing the executive with group support; 360-degree feedback is also a way of providing impact information. Fundamentally, however, the individual must make a conscious choice to begin the journey and shift his or her behavior for the good of the business.

Committing to Success

It is interesting to observe those occasions when people quit even though they know they should not. Sometimes people quit when they believe they "must" change or when there is too much pressure on them to change. Resistance is a natural response to any type of pressure, particularly if you have already made many changes in order to get to the top of the corporate structure. People also quit when they are taken out of their comfort zone. This assumes that business growth and change should be comfortable. They aren't. We cannot expect to compete in an increasingly competitive market by continuing to hold on to the status quo. Long-term success will not come to those who just work harder; rather, it will come to those who confront their worst fears, refuse to quit, and break through their own self-imposed limitations to achieve a new level of performance.

The fundamental commitment to succeed must be there and so must the willingness to give up the past and be challenged by the future. Leadership for integrity requires a lot of work. It is not a function to be performed by someone who is retired on the job or looking to cash out in the company's next early retirement option. To deal with these disconnects, it is important that leadership commit to following through on the process and ensuring its success.

The Business and Customer Focus

By definition, change processes tend to focus the energy of the workforce internally. This can have a significant impact on customer satisfaction and confidence in the company. The focus on building value for the new work environment can also shift energy and attention away from the completion of current priorities. In addition, anxiety about what will take the place of hierarchy can undermine the shift to the collaborative team-based organization.

It is essential to manage the transition to the new work ethic carefully, keeping priorities clear, maintaining balance, and not dropping the ball on existing commitments.

Remembering the Customer

One possible disconnect during the change process is that we may forget the customer as we focus our energy on realigning the organization internally. Even if customers are warned about what is happening inside the company, we do not want to shake their confidence in our ability to continue delivering top-quality products and services. Whatever happens in the change process, we must remember the customer at all times. It may be as simple as keeping the issue in front of the workforce at every meeting or posting banners, or it may require a more in-depth process of building a measurement system to track progress on a weekly or monthly basis.

Throughout the process, the question needs to be asked: "How will this affect our customers? How will this action affect our quality?" In a work environment where everyone is a customer, these questions apply equally to those inside the company. A "hit squad" can be created to respond to specific customers' issues as they arise, and be given the authority to make interventions to maintain customer satisfaction.

The company can integrate the full-value contracting process into the change effort, as discussed in Chapter 5. The entire organization can be engaged in establishing quality standards that will be used to measure the value of its products and services and its relationships with customers. This process can be tied in to existing total quality work or to the strategic alignment process.

Frustration With Slow Buy-In

Time is of the essence in any change process. The collaborative approach, however, requires a high level of buy-in from across the organization at the same time that it requires urgent action. A disconnect can occur if management gets so frustrated with the slow pace of buy-in that it moves forward without it, or if the process is not fully implemented. One conclusion the workforce may draw from this is that the results are predetermined. At such a point, the credibility of the effort can be damaged.

To address this dilemma, the dynamics of the buy-in process must be clearly understood. Set realistic expectations for all aspects of the change, including the strategic redirection of the business. For example, achieving workforce buy-in to a strategic redirection in an organization of 1,000 people may take six to twelve months. Keep the business moving forward using the multiple-track process discussed earlier.

A third way to respond to the time issue is to agree on what early visible successes will be delivered in a 60- to 90-day time frame. In one financial services company where this approach was used, a target of $40 million invested in 90 days was established at the beginning of the process. Not only did the goal bring everyone together around a common business purpose, but they exceeded the goal by 250 percent, establishing a platform for credibility that carried them well along toward their second financial goal.

What Do We Do With the Hierarchy?

Some companies find themselves in a conflict between their commitment to collaboration and the traditional structures that have served them so well all these years. A disconnect can occur if the workforce comes to believe that collaboration is being used merely as another technique to increase productivity rather than as the basis for a new cultural framework. Communicating—using symbols and press releases—is not enough. Putting the hierarchy to rest must be a visible and ongoing process.

There needs to be a specific road map for the change process that is clear to everyone. Post it at the employee entrances to work. Chart your progress on that map. Put everyone on a team early in the process. Get them basic skills training. Begin to make visible changes in the human resources function by redesigning the performance appraisal and compensation systems to reflect the values of the Collaborative Workplace. Measure your effectiveness every six months. Celebrate the accomplishment of your milestones.

Make this change process as real and practical as possible for everyone, in places where it is important.

Workforce Relationships and Processes

In creating a Collaborative Workplace, we are transforming mindsets, behaviors, and our approach to all aspects of how we lead and manage the workplace from command-and-control to collaboration. Defining and implementing the new covenant takes time and patience. It requires vigilance in applying the methodology and a commitment to learn from our mistakes.

In this change process, disconnects in work relationships and communications among management and the workforce can occur regularly. With uncertainty and skepticism come anxiety, tension, and stress. There is no place to hide. We need a strategy to address several frequent disconnects in this arena.

"I'm From Missouri"

"Assume I'm from Missouri, the show-me state. You show me why I should buy into this approach." The workforce is routinely subjected to the entire spectrum of training and organization development interventions designed to make them better and more productive as people, workers, or professionals. In many instances, senior management does not participate. As one vice president said about a leadership development seminar, "Our hope is that by osmosis we will get the needed change in our culture. We expect it to happen if there is a critical mass that completes this training." There wasn't and it didn't. In fact the training was cut in half because the intended implementation value was not being realized.

Considerable skepticism can result when people feel they are being treated like guinea pigs, especially if top management does not itself participate. Resistance and resentment greet each newcomer on the scene as more and more people end up in the "Missouri" mind-set. In the creation and management of the Collaborative Workplace, the burden of proof is on management to demonstrate its commitment to the process. As we have said, collaboration is a way of life. Managers can invest themselves in building a new type of working relationship with those in the trenches. They can become involved with the workforce on the shop floor or in the cubicles to build and sustain value for the new work environment.

Similarly, it is vital that the workforce be actively engaged with management in defining the new covenant that will articulate the new expectations each party has of the other, their mutual responsibilities, and the benefits each derives from this new relationship. In addition, members must be involved in the process of redefining the work culture, using the Operating Agreements process in work teams of all kinds as the primary vehicle for doing so. This process will allow the collaborative culture to emerge across the organization rather than being imposed on it from above.

Doing Real Work

Another significant disconnect for employees occurs when they have so little value for the change process that they consider it to be separate and distinct from their real jobs. At one information systems organization that experienced the "Missouri" mind-set, it was believed that unless you were key-punching codes into the computer, you were not doing real work. Attendance at team meetings was considered a waste of time, especially if they focused on team games or nonquantitative process stuff. People usually value what they own. Give the workforce ownership of the change process so that they can realize its value. One way to do this is to build collaborative teams around real business issues that require a solution within a given time frame. Real work in real time by real teams builds value.

Building Tolerance for Ambiguity

The regional manager of the distribution center was overheard on his conference call with the main office: "Are you telling me I no longer have my title and that I have two bosses, one of whom is a coach?" Most of us have a very difficult time with this transition to a flat work environment where we are all more or less equal, and where traditional bosses who once told us what to do have been turned into coaches with unclear responsibilities. Who tells me what to do? Who does my performance evaluation?

This can seem like an ambiguous work environment, and it doesn't feel good. The disconnects occur when members "dial out" in terms of their energy level because the new work relationships have not been sufficiently clarified. People will tend not to commit to something that they do not understand or that threatens their economic survival.

We could, of course, begin telling them what to do. On the other hand, we could engage them in a process of taking responsibility for their own futures, the workplace, and their jobs. Start the collaborative team formation process. Create Operating Agreements. Establish milestones and create action plans to achieve them.

In the Collaborative Workplace, everyone takes full responsibility for the success of the enterprise. The only job security is what the team creates for itself by meeting its customers' needs with superior-quality products and services. The reality is that we now *have* to operate in an ambiguous work environment. Stability is gone. Cycle time continues to collapse, and time expectations from customers are becoming less forgiving. Quality expectations are going up, and cost pressures mean our jobs continue to be redefined. What *will* remain constant is the collaborative culture we create for ourselves, because values and principles tend to remain constant over time.

Developing New Skills

The challenge of creating the new workplace is often greater than we realize at the time we commit to it. Sometimes we ask our people to do things they do not have the skills to do. For example, a manufacturing vice president told his direct reports that in the new self-directed work environment they were no longer supervisors but facilitators. The managers didn't know how to facilitate. The result was a group of frustrated managers who didn't feel up to the task and a workforce that was confused about their new relationship with the managers.

It is critical to the success of the Collaborative Workplace that the people entrusted with its creation and management feel confident in their new roles. We need to clearly identify their roles and responsibilities and the new skills they will require to be successful and then provide them the opportunity to get that training. Leaders need to know how to be facilitators, coaches, and catalysts for change. They need to learn how to design and facilitate meetings, form and manage collaborative teams, make strategic interventions to resolve conflicts, manage problem-solving techniques, and enable the change process to be successful. With an effective level of proficiency in these skills, they can identify breaks in the integrity of the change process and work to ensure its overall success.

Organization Systems

To ensure the permanence of the collaborative work ethic, these values need to be reflected in all the internal organization systems and processes. The human resource, finance, legal, administration, and information systems are fundamental to the day-to-day operations of any business. It is in these systems that transformational change can be the most difficult. But without a fundamental shift in their operation, the entire change process can be undercut.

For example, in one company, the sales force organized itself as a collaborative team and developed a very aggressive marketing program. Having decided that incentive pay would go to the team as a whole, not to individuals, they wanted it to be divided equally among the members on a quarterly basis. The finance office at headquarters, however, had a time-honored tradition of paying only individuals and had a formula for the level of pay they would receive. When the sales team produced a sales level 50 percent above the original target, its members did not get paid in accordance with the system they had agreed to internally. The result was a major disconnect between finance and sales, with recriminations and bad feelings both ways. Sales was trying out the new values and thought it was making them real by creating a group incentive. Finance thought it was doing its job, and because it had been given no instructions to the contrary, did not understand why everyone was so upset.

This type of disconnect can happen many times over as the

organization implements collaborative values. How should new values be reflected in new systems? Who is responsible for making the change? What impacts will these systems changes have on the effectiveness of the organization? Here are some possible disconnects and some ways to resolve them.

Becoming Focused on the Internal Customer

In a chemicals company, the corporate information systems group was known for being very internally focused—working to refine the perfect software application, even though the business units had not even asked for it. E-mail communications were the primary vehicles by which this highly networked organization functioned, but unfortunately there were four different systems to choose from. Fundamentally the organization's information networks were incompatible, duplicative, and inaccessible. The IS help desk seemed to never be available when it was needed. All across the company, professionals began acquiring their own PCs, building their own applications from off-the-shelf software packages, and basically withdrawing their support for the information systems group. It was small wonder when two years later the IS group was decentralized into the business units.

In moving to a collaborative work environment, a central, driving value is focusing the business on the customer. This same value applies internally. Organization systems groups can increase their short-term value to the business by initiating their own customer engagement process with their internal partners. In this process they open up their policies and procedures to the scrutiny and constructive criticism of their customers, ask for improvements and enhancements, and identify specific things the customers want to get handled in the next 90 days. Then they meet those needs and provide those services. Finally, they begin building longer-term value by developing full-value contracts with those customers.

The integrity of the transition to a Collaborative Workplace requires that we build relationship and value rather than erect barriers to effective and efficient operations. Ultimately, the value any systems group brings to the table is the service it can offer its customers so their customers can achieve high performance.

Moving From Control to Contribution

A major role for many organization systems groups is control: of expenditures, of hiring and firing, of compensation and benefits, of contracting, procurement, and legal actions. Control can become a mind-set of the people who have been trained to maintain it. Organizationally, they have been grouped together in silos that, in many instances, have become isolated from the mainstream of the business. Issues of responsiveness and accountability are often the result.

If these organizations are to become effective partners in the Collaborative Workplace, they need to focus much more on building work relationships that bring value to their internal customers. This may require a shift in mind-set and behavior. It may also require new work processes and new ways of providing services. Specifically, the change team can engage the leadership of the systems groups as a special project team that undertakes a specific assessment of work relationships and business processes with each of the line organizations. Above all, there needs to be a realignment of systems organizations from control to contribution and service.

Realigning Organization Systems

Old habits die hard, and old value systems almost never die. They are ingrained in our minds like icons, sacred cows that may never be touched. In one company, the presidential awards had become a hollow shell that often rewarded competitive rather than team behavior. Incentive and bonus pay was given to individuals. Efforts to replace this system with team-based awards were resisted. Some members of teams concluded that their team activities would have to wait until they completed the work essential to getting their bonus pay. The result was that several teams disbanded.

The Collaborative Workplace is open, providing the freedom to determine what processes, systems, or approaches are still needed, based on principle, on what is best for the customer, and on their congruence with the core values of the collaboration. Systems may be redesigned to support the needs of the customer and the new culture.

Creating a Healing Culture

In organizations that are experiencing the culture wars, healing is essential. It helps to create an environment in which these types of issues can be openly discussed. What follows are some suggestions that indicate what a collaborative organization can do to help create a healing culture. If your organization has already done these things, the suggestions may provide a platform for further expansion.

Cross-functional teams can review the organizational support systems to ensure that they bring value to the customer and the workforce. This collaborative values review can recommend the redesign of specific functions, which can then be streamlined and simplified. Responsibility for the day-to-day management of the systems functions can be delegated to collaborative teams. For example, the teams could hire and train their own members.

In human resources, the personnel ladder and performance review processes can be replaced with a 360-degree feedback system, results-based performance awards, and decentralized responsibility for team-based reviews. Appraisals can be based both on individual and on team performance. Career and professional development can be based on the needs of the customer, and skills development can be directly related to the enhancement of customer-based skills.

Information systems can have an architecture driven by customer requirements. The internal communications system can become more user-friendly. Information systems staff can have their appraisals tied to customer satisfaction.

In the finance, administration, and legal divisions, the project management system can be simplified to focus on meeting customer requirements. Budget and financial reporting systems can be put on-line, simplified, and made user-friendly.

Summary

After the prenuptial agreements have been signed and the honeymoon is over, the hard work begins in managing the transition to a Collaborative Workplace. In the first year or so after the process is initiated, many if not all of these disconnects are likely to occur. The real question is not when they will appear, but how the organization will manage the integrity of the processes, methods, and tools when they do. There is no set game plan. There is no preset strategy. The leadership processes in a Collaborative Workplace, however, must always come from principle, from the core values of the Collaborative Work Ethic, if they are to be successful.

The temptation to lapse into old behavior is enormous. It is like the rites of passage for a young man who must face down his enemies and inner fears as he searches for his soul in the man he already is. Managing the evolution of the Collaborative Workplace is very much like this. The core values and beliefs are already there—resident in the people who work in the organization. But in maturing to a position of full responsibility for their future, they must face their fears together, look into the mirror to see what is there, and be willing to persevere through the difficult times so that they may realize their full value, their dignity, and their self-respect.

Epilogue

Any company that hopes to be competitive in the 21st century may want to consider creating a Collaborative Workplace. In these times of instability and chaos, it is not only the most efficient form of organization for a highly networked marketplace, but also the most effective way to engage the members of the workforce and enable them to be their most productive selves. Even more important, it brings dignity, civility, and values-based stability to the workplace.

The past, however, is no longer prologue. We cannot create the future by reengineering the past. To forge a new path into the 21st century, we must now seize the opportunity to transcend our current way of thinking about leading and managing businesses. The intention of this book has been to define that pathway.

It is time to stop looking for the silver bullet to resolve complex organizational issues. It is time to move beyond the quick fix. It is time to truly transform our organizations, to face the paradox head-on, and to bring peace and healing into the workplace. It is time for us to exercise a conscious choice, and to act from our integrity and what we know is right about how to treat people in the workplace.

Let's go to work!

Appendix

Sample Operating Agreements

A. Decision Making: Consensus

Consensus means that we will talk through things until everyone can support the decision. If not, we can:

- Postpone the decision.
- Do additional fact-finding.
- Get a verbal yes or no.
- Put it on the next agenda.

- Consensus leads to a win-win.
- Team needs to recognize which decisions to postpone or not postpone.

  - Team reaches consensus on whether to decide or postpone.
  - If it can't be put off, keep discussing until we get consensus; the relationship is more important than the decision.

- If I disagree, I will share my reasons.

  - Team will make an effort to address them.
  - If I still have a reservation, I will let the team know.

- If I disagree, I will listen and try to be open.

Note: These are actual notes from a meeting of a team's Operating Agreements, and do not represent a complete set. No two sets of Agreements are the same. These are not intended for actual use by a team.

- Be flexible.
- Consider changing.
- Back off—identify where we are in agreement.
- Look for alternatives.

- I will be open in any situation.
- When a decision is reached, I feel others have respected my opinion; I like the way I got treated.
- If I disagree, I will be empathetic in my listening and look for the real issue.
- I will be willing to take the time to address the real issue.

B. Responsibility

- I will take responsibility not to speak up now.
- We are willing to test the waters, to take a risk.

    - To be heard, not ignored.
    - To not feel repercussions later.
    - To not be steamrolled.

- These meetings are our meetings.

    - I am responsible for the success of this meeting.
    - I need to be aware of how my behavior impacts the meeting.

- When there is gossip or triangulation in a conflict situation and I am asked to join, I can:

    - Refuse to participate.
    - Police myself.
    - Refer the individual(s) back to the team.
    - Contact the resource.

- Question for clarity.

C. Intentionality

- Shared intention for one another's success.
- We will create a successful collaborative environment that produces superior results.

D. *Attendance*

- Mandatory unless an emergency—family or medical.
- Schedule in advance to ensure all can attend.
- Notify contact ASAP about an emergency.
- Can cancel meeting.
- When there is an emergency, individual is briefed before next meeting and at next meeting has a chance to comment, upgrade.
- If more than one person has an emergency, contact will decide whether to have the meeting or not.

E. *"Safety"*

- "Safety" means psychological safety.
- Keep the good of the team in mind.
- No retribution—have faith there will be none.
- We are anchored in common goal.

    - Those with rank empower others and walk the talk.
    - Others take the risk that "rankers" mean it.

- We will take the time to work things through; the relationship comes first even when our plates are full.
- Be sensitive to others when wanting to help.
- Adhere to the Operating Agreements.
- Be self-observant.
- We will not hold every disagreement to be a basis for peer ranking.
- Focus on the issue and not on the individual.
- Avoid being obnoxious in disagreements.
- Take judicious breaks.
- Fun is OK as long as it doesn't hurt someone else.
- Have faith that honest disagreements and participating will be rewarded.

F. *Accountability*

- We will protect the integrity of the process. In a one-on-one situation, where there is a problem, I can:

- Hear, talk, and bury it.
- Refer the person back to the team.
- Refer the person to the resource.
- Jointly decide how I want to handle it; team versus friend.
- Individually be accountable to the team for my actions outside the meeting.
- Check it out if I think someone is violating the Operating Agreements.
- Explain my actions to the team when I am concerned about how they might be construed.
- If there is an exception, bring it to the team for agreement.

G. Confidentiality

- Meeting memory is not passed around; if you don't want something in the memory, flag it.

  - Our document; no copies.
  - Reference documents in conversations.
  - List confidential items on last page.

H. Communications

- Share with people where we are in the process—Action Plan.
- Agree on the message.
- Tolerate ambiguity:

  - Be willing to invest time to delve into an area or revisit an area or decision even though you may not want to.
  - Recognize that this will happen.
  - Recognize that this process takes time; trust the process.
  - Our intent:

    - Not to mislead people—no passing around meeting memories (see Confidentiality).
    - No passing out of partial information that other people may interpret themselves.

- No presenting our opinions when they may not represent those of the team.

I. Forgiveness

- Have patience.
- We will cut one another some slack.

J. Amendment

- It is OK to amend the Operating Agreements at any time in a manner consistent with our consensus decision-making rule.

K. Openness

- Use judgment on processing issues.
- Shared interest.
- Be willing to take risks about issues under discussion: risk of backfiring; risk of too many alternatives.
- Be open unless an Operating Agreement triggers something.
- Encourage one another to be open.
- Long-term intent to create an open or collaborative environment.

L. Operations

- OK to stand up, move around the room.
- Always bring calendars.
- E-mail communications—copy one another on anything that impacts the team.
- Do memories electronically if at all possible.
- We will have a contact to handle our meetings on a three-month rotation.

Selected Readings

Belasco, James A. *Teaching the Elephant to Dance, The Manager's Guide to Empowering Change*. New York: Penguin Group, 1991.

Bleeke, Joel, and David Ernst, eds. *Collaborating to Compete: Using Strategic Alliances and Acquisitions in the Global Marketplace*. New York: Wiley, 1993.

Covey, Steven. *The Seven Habits of Highly Effective People*. New York: Simon & Schuster, 1989.

DePree, Max. *Leadership Is an Art*. New York: Doubleday, 1989.

Drucker, Peter F. *The New Realities*. New York: Harper & Row, 1989.

Jaffe, Dennis T., Cynthia D. Scott, and Glenn R. Tobe. *Rekindling Commitment*. San Francisco: Jossey-Bass, 1994.

Kanter, Rosabeth Moss, Barry A. Stein, and Todd D. Jick. *The Challenge of Organizational Change*. New York: The Free Press, 1992.

Kearns, David T., and David A. Nadler, *Prophets in the Dark*. New York: HarperBusiness, 1992.

Kilmann, Ralph H. *Beyond the Quick Fix*. San Francisco: Jossey-Bass, 1991.

Kochan, Thomas A., and Michael Useem. *Transforming Organizations*. New York: Oxford University Press, 1992.

Nirenberg, John. *The Living Organization, Transforming Teams Into Workplace Communities*. Homewood, Ill.: Business One Irwin, and San Diego: Pfeiffer & Company, 1993.

Peck, M. Scott. *A World Waiting to Be Born: Civility Rediscovered*. New York: Bantam Books, 1993.

Rosen, Robert H. *The Healthy Company, Eight Strategies to Develop People, Productivity, and Profits*. New York: Jeremy Tarcher/Peregee Books, 1991.

Savage, Charles M. *Fifth-Generation Management*. Digital Press, 1990.

Schein, Edgar H. *Organizational Culture and Leadership*. San Francisco: Jossey-Bass, 1991.

Schrage, Michael, *Shared Minds: The New Technologies of Collaboration*. New York: Random House, 1990.

Senge, Peter M. *The Fifth Discipline*. New York: Doubleday, 1990.

Index